WEST SUSSEX

This book is issued for three
be returned on or be...
below

10 152 3437

THE MOUNTAINS OF IRELAND

1 Errigal and the Derryveagh mountains

The MOUNTAINS of IRELAND

D. D. C. Pochin Mould
B.SC., PH.D.

GILL AND MACMILLAN

First published 1955

This second edition
published 1976 by

Gill & Macmillan Limited
15/17 Eden Quay
Dublin 1
and internationally through
association with the
Macmillan Publishers Group

© D. D. C. Pochin Mould, 1955, 1976

7171 0815 5

Printed and bound in Great Britain by
REDWOOD BURN LIMITED
Trowbridge & Esher

PREFACE TO THE SECOND EDITION

It is now many years since I first got to know the Irish hills and wrote *The Mountains of Ireland*. The book has been out of print for a long time too, though still often asked for. In the intervening period, I have got to know the Irish hills even more intimately, both from walking and from flying over them. This new edition, whilst retaining the original text, adds the fruit of this further experience in that the pictures are all new and most of them are my own aerial photographs. In fact, only from the air can the full beauty and shape of the hills be properly seen—and for the walker and climber, the exact details of routes up them.

When I first wrote this book, I could say that mountaineering and hill walking in Ireland was still a young sport. It is hardly that now, for more and more people are taking to the hills. On the lower slopes, the forest parks with their nature trails, attract many visitors. Wild life and the countryside are increasingly appreciated. So, if I described the first edition as a signpost to the hills, then so unknown, this present one is rather in the nature of a book to tell more about mountains already sought for, known and loved.

D.D.C.P.M.
June 1976

ACKNOWLEDGMENT

All the photographs in this edition of *The Mountains of Ireland* are by the author, with the exception of numbers 24, 25, 30 and 38, which are from the photo library of the Northern Ireland Tourist Board, Belfast, and numbers 26 and 31, from that of Bord Fáilte, Dublin. Author and publisher would like to express their thanks for permission to use these pictures.

CONTENTS

		Page
Preface		7
Acknowledgment		8
List of Illustrations		11
Sources		13

CHAPTER
I	THE MOUNTAINS OF IRELAND	15
II	CONNEMARA	28
III	SLIGO AND DONEGAL	47
IV	THE BURREN	67
V	THE HEIGHT OF ERIN	76
VI	THE LEINSTER CHAIN	89
VII	THE KINGDOM OF MOURNE	102
VIII	GALTEE AND COMERAGH	119
IX	WEST CORK AND KERRY	130
X	MOUNT BRANDON AND CARRAUNTUAL	145
	Index	157

LIST OF ILLUSTRATIONS

The numerals in parentheses in the text refer to the *figure numbers* of the illustrations, and not to page numbers.

Figure		Page
1	Errigal and the Derryveagh mountains	*Frontispiece*
2	Sketch map of the Mountains of Ireland	14
3	Caher, Carrauntual and Beenkeragh in winter	21
4	Beenkeragh, Carrauntual and Caher in early spring	21
5	Curraghs on Inisheer with the Maumturks in the distance	22
6	Coumshingaun in the Comeragh mountains	22
7	The Connemara mountains. Glen Inagh, with the Twelve Bens, Mweelrea and the Maumturk mountains	29
8	Croagh Patrick and the pilgrim path to the summit chapel	30
9	The Glen of the Downs and the Great Sugar Loaf, Co. Wicklow	30
10	The Maumturks, Co. Galway	39
11	The Twelve Bens, Co. Galway	39
12	Killary Harbour, Ireland's only fiord, Co. Mayo	40
13	Mweelrea (2,688 feet), Co. Mayo	40
14	The ridge of Errigal, Co. Donegal	49
15	The stone fort of Grianan of Ailech in Donegal	50
16	Altan Lough and the Aghla More-Muckish ridge	50
17	The ridge and sea cliffs of Slieve League, Co. Donegal	59
18	Ben Bulben, Co. Sligo	60
19	The skyline of the Donegal hills including Errigal	60
20	Cloudscape over the Mourne mountains	69
21	Sunset over Galway Bay and the hills of the Burren	69
22	Typical Burren country—Mullagh More, Co. Clare	70
23	The early Christian stone 'fort' of Cahercommaun in the Burren	70
24	Glenariff, one of the 'Glens of Antrim'	79

LIST OF ILLUSTRATIONS

25	Slieve Gullion and its forest park, Co. Armagh	80
26	The Slieve Bloom mountains	80
27	Fossil ripple prints in Old Red Sandstone rocks on the ridge of the Macgillycuddy Reeks, Co. Kerry	85
28	Pattern of hill farms on the slopes of the Paps of Dana, Co. Kerry	85
29	The Sperrin mountains	86
30	Slemish, the hill of St. Patrick's captivity, Co. Antrim	86
31	Lugnaquillia and Glenmalure, Co. Wicklow	95
32	The Slieve Mish and the hill fort of Caherconree, Co. Kerry	95
33	Glendalough, Co. Wicklow	96
34	Mount Brandon, Co. Kerry	96
35	The eastern cliffs under the summit of Mount Brandon, Co. Kerry	105
36	The Mountains of Mourne	106–7
37	The Upper Lake and Macgillycuddy Reeks, Killarney	108
38	The Silent Valley reservoir in the Mourne Mountains, Co. Down	109
39	Ridge and corrie lake on the mountain line from Carrauntual to Coomakista and Waterville, Co. Kerry	121
40	The Galtee mountains from the south	122
41	The lake and forest park of Gougane Barra, Co. Cork	131
42	The Healy Pass, on the Cork/Kerry border	132
43	The hills of the Beara peninsula with Glanbeg lough and (extreme right) Hungry Hill	137
44	Mangerton, Killarney in winter with the head of the Horses' Glen and the Devil's Punch Bowl	138
45	Mangerton in summer with the distant view to the Lower Lake at Killarney	138
46	The Pedlar's lake, Connor Pass, Co. Kerry	147
47	The Macgillycuddy Reeks, Co. Kerry	148
48	The Gap of Dunloe, Co. Kerry	148

SOURCES

Very little has, as yet, been written about the Irish mountains as such. But as sources of information about Ireland as a whole, its geology, geography, history, etc., I list the following books, in which, naturally, there is a considerable amount of information about the hills themselves.

CHARLESWORTH, J. K. *The Geology of Ireland.* Edinburgh, 1953.

COLEMAN, J. C. *The Mountains of Killarney.* Dundalk, 1948.

CORKERY, DANIEL. *The Fortunes of the Irish Language.* Dublin, 1954.

CURTIS, EDMUND. *A History of Ireland.* London, 1936.

FREEMAN, T. W. *Ireland. Its physical, historical, social and economic geography.* London, 1950.

EVANS, E. ESTYN. *Irish Heritage.* Dundalk, 1942.
Mourne Country. Dundalk, 1951.

Ó RIORDÁIN, SEÁN P. *Antiquities of the Irish Countryside.* London, 1953.

PRAEGAR, R. LLOYD. *Irish Landscape.* Dublin, 1954.
Natural History of Ireland. London, 1950.
The Botanist in Ireland. Dublin, 1934.

WALL, C. W. *Mountaineering in Ireland.* Dublin, 1939. (A brief account of the main routes up all the Irish hills.)

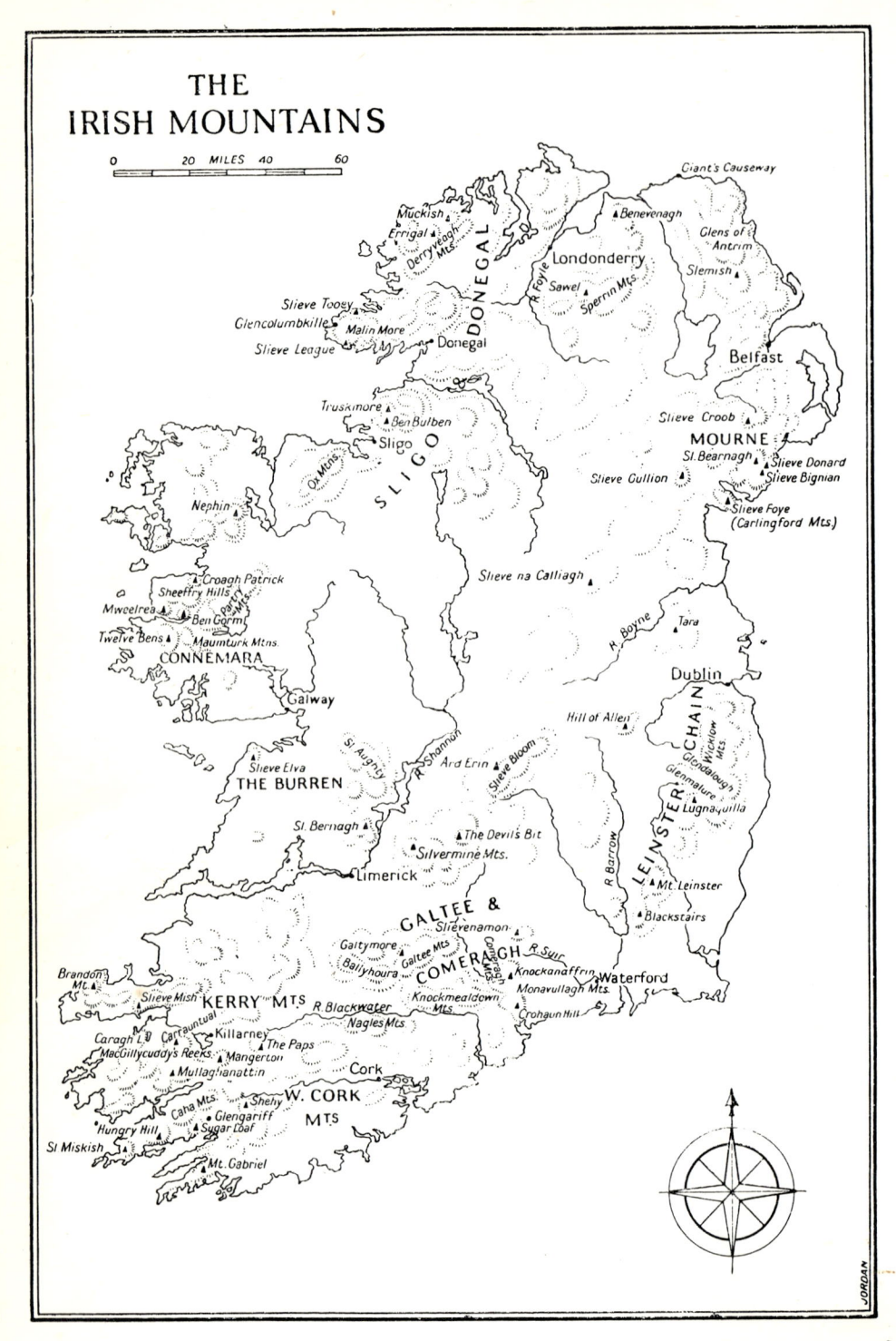

2 Sketch map of the mountains of Ireland

CHAPTER I

The Mountains of Ireland

It is not of mountains that the stranger thinks when he imagines Ireland; not the bare rock, the driven snow, the dark lake cradled in the lonely corrie; rather of something green and pastoral. Yet, for the Irishman himself, the mountains rising blue in the distance across the level brown of the peat bogs or the green of the undulating fields, form an essential part of his picture of his country. His mind turns upon little hills that rise from the plains and carry in their very names the sound of history: Uisneach the ancient centre of Erin, Tara, Saul, of St. Patrick's first church, Cashel, of the Kings; and then to those girdling chains of real mountains that rise like dragon's teeth around the rim of the island and whose slopes were both the homesteads of the first Irish farmers and the last unyielding bastion of Irish culture.

For Ireland is ringed with hills: the Mournes in the north-east (Slieve Donard, 2796 feet)(36), the Wicklows in the east (Lugnaquillia, 3039 feet)(31), the Galtees and Comeraghs in the south (Galtymore, 3018 feet)(40), the Kerry mountains in the south-west (Carrauntual, 3414 feet, Ireland's highest top)(47), the Burren (Slieve Elva, 1134 feet) (23) and Connemara (Mweelrea, 2688 feet)(13) in the west, and the Donegal hills in the north-west (Errigal, 2466 feet)(14). And each of these groups is not only real mountain country, but has its own particular and unique personality and character. To climb in Ireland is to range from limestone "karst" to granite torr, from bare and slippery quartzite to springy downland turf and mighty cliffs of red and violet sandstone.

Two things only have these diverse groups of mountains in common, an immediate and intimate relationship between the rocks of which they are built and the nature and form of the hills themselves, and the nearness of the sea. Except for the

Galtees, the principal Irish mountain chains are set close upon the sea and the winds that strike them are salted with the ocean; the climber looks down not only on the checkerboard pattern of fields below but on the ridges of the waves and on alternating cliff and strand, and out to islands whose stories are interwoven with the stream of Irish history. It is not only the mountains of Mourne that sweep down to the sea; all of them combine the splendour of the heights with the splendour of the depths, and their summit cairns have something of the wistful magic of the Brendan legend, of the saint climbing a high mountain and looking out upon the boundless ocean and glimpsing the earthly paradise far out on the western horizon.

Statistics bring home the fact that their actual area does not necessarily indicate the importance of the Irish mountains in either landscape or history. Three-quarters of Ireland lies below the 500-foot contour and actual mountain land only makes up 11 per cent of the surface area. Only 5 per cent of Ireland is over 1000 feet and only 1/400th above 2000 feet. The highest point, the 3414 feet of Carrauntual, is in the Kerry hills, low by mountain standards outside of Ireland, yet since there is nothing higher by which they may be dwarfed, the Irish mountains rear themselves up into the clouds in what sometimes appears an almost alpine majesty, steep sloped and rocky, and sometimes in winter, with snow cornices flashing against the deep and vivid blue of the Irish sky.

In general, one may say that the Irish hills are built of harder and more resistant rocks than the Carboniferous limestone that underlies most of the great central plain of Ireland. In the west, however, in Burren and near Sligo, the limestones themselves form upland, bleak "karst" in Burren and precipice-bounded mountains at Sligo. Then, too, the "grain" of the hills has been determined by ancient earth movements which crumpled the rocks along particular lines of folding and compression; and the final moulding of the hills was brought about by the ice of the glacial period.

Apart from the Lewisian gneiss of the little island of Inishtrahull, it is in the west that the most ancient rocks of Ireland are to be found. The Connemara mountains are built partly of ancient rocks—quartzite, granite, the beautiful green striped Connemara marble, the hard quartzites forming the hill ridges—

THE GEOLOGY OF THE HILLS

and date back to the pre-Cambrian, the earliest geological period recognised. In Donegal, the high tops are again of resistant quartzite, but of somewhat later Dalradian Age, the continuation across into Ireland of the schists and quartzites of the Central Highlands of Scotland. The quartzite tops of Errigal, the Poisoned Glen and the like are echoed over in Scotland in the symmetrical Paps of Jura and the heights of Islay. The great Scottish fault lines, of the Great Glen, the Highland Boundary and the Southern Upland Boundary can be traced across into Ireland, together with the rocks which they affect.

The Wicklow mountains are composed of granite; so too the Mournes, but of much later (Tertiary) date than the Leinster hills. In the south, the Galtees, Knockmealdowns and Comeraghs and the hills of Kerry are composed of the sandstones of the Old Red Sandstone period, with massive crags of violet and purple rock.

The north then continues the pattern of the Scottish hills and the grain of the country follows the same NE.–SW. direction imposed by the Caledonian orogen (mountain building movement) which preceded the Carboniferous period. But as you go south in Ireland the direction imposed by the folding changes and the southern hills are controlled by the east–west trend of the post-Carboniferous Hercynian orogen (named from the Hartz mountains, also called Armorican from the old name for Brittany). In Ireland, these two great structural lines of Europe meet: they finally intersect across the Atlantic in the Appalachians.

In the Ice Age the whole of Ireland, except for some small areas in the south-west, seems to have been overwhelmed by the great ice sheets. The hilltops were rounded and smoothed, except for the highest Kerry tops which still rose above the sea of ice. Later, as the cold lessened and the great sheets of ice retreated, the Irish hills still nourished their own snowfields and glaciers and deep corries were plucked out in their crag faces as the ice gathered there and moved outward to the valleys below.

The small ice-free districts are important not only in providing the rock-climber with splintered crags for his amusement, but in leaving a small foothold where some plants and animals could survive the cold. Not all life became extinct, and part of the Irish flora and fauna seems almost certainly a pre-glacial relict one, though the bulk of it is a recolonisation across then existing land-bridges in the wake of the retreating ice.

Up the west coast then, in Kerry, Connemara and Donegal, are to be found, often in quantity, two special and very interesting groups of plants, one linked with Western Europe and one with North America. The North American group is the less interesting of the two; its presence suggests an earlier, closer linkage between Ireland and America by land-bridges and is paralleled by some European species along the east coast of America. It includes *Spiranthes gemmipara* and *S. stricta* (lady's tresses), the blue-eyed grass (*Sisyrinchium angustifolium*) and the rushes *Juncus macer* and *J. dudleyi*.

In the Lusitanean Mediterranean group are not only delightful flowers, but a small corresponding group of molluscs, beetles, woodlice and earthworms. Both may well have survived the Ice Age in the ice-free areas. The plants include the famous arbutus, the lovely deep violet butterwort of the Kerry bogs (*Pinquicula grandiflora*), four heaths (*Erica mediterranea, mackii, ciliaris* and *vagans*) and St. Dabeoc's heath (*Dabeocia polifolia*), the orchid *Neotinea intacta*, and the saxifrages—*Saxifraga spathularis* (St. Patrick's cabbage, a close relative of the London pride) and *S. geum*. The arbutus is to be found in the hillside woods of the Killarney mountains and among the hills of Sligo: place-names indicate that it once occurred in intermediate stations up the west coast. The Irish name of the arbutus is *cuinche*, which is found in place-names as Quin and Quinsheen—an island in Clew Bay. The Mediterranean heath tinges the Nephin mountains pale purple with its blossom in early spring; whilst St. Dabeoc's heath, with large pink bells and glossy green foliage silvered on the underside, is one of the glories of Connemara, in flower there from June until nearly Christmas-time.

Then, too, the climber on the Irish hills will delight in the special limestone-loving plants of Burren and the Ben Bulben hills of Sligo, and in the small collection of alpines to be found on Irish crags and cliffs. The mild wet Irish climate, lacking lingering snowfields, is not ideal for alpine plants, and accordingly they are to be found not so much on the actual summits but on the cliffs facing north and at levels ranging from 1000 to 1500 feet above sea-level. In fact, "alpines" can be found growing right down to sea-level. The link between sea and hill extends even to the small plants of the mountainside.

As the ice retreated and the climate improved, forests spread up the Irish hillsides. On the very summits you will see the stumps of pines marking forest layers in the peat. The pine itself died out naturally about the time the first men arrived, around 2000 B.C. or earlier, and the picture of that time is of dense wood and bogland on the low ground, with woodland alternating with grassy sward on the higher levels. Oak was, and is, the dominant native tree, with birches on the hills and alders in the swamps, and with yew and holly and hazel. The first settlers beach-combed along the shores, later came the Megalithic people, farmers, traders, sailors, with a custom of burying their dead in great chambered tombs. They settled on the dry uplands where the light soil could be easily worked and their cattle find pasture. From that time on the woods of Ireland began to diminish, by the browsing of young seedlings by cattle and sheep, by felling for agricultural reclamation, or for building or iron smelting, and, apparently on a large scale, to destroy cover in which one's enemy might lurk. The Irish hills today are treeless places for the most part, except for the Killarney woods and the new plantations of State Forestry schemes. The old extent of wood can be traced in place-names, the *Derry* that means an oak wood (*daire*) and *coille*, wood (as in Kylemore—great wood).

So as you climb up you make almost a cross-section of history, leaving behind modern Ireland in the valley, and on the high slopes coming upon Megalithic chambered tombs and standing stones, and, numerous on the very summits, the massive circular burial cairns of the slightly later Bronze Age people. Here and there old mine-workings appear to go back to the first utilisation of metals in Ireland, and the glitter of Irish gold in the museum collections is a reminder of men long ago panning the gravels of the mountain streams.

As the ground was progressively cleared for cultivation and habitation, the settlements moved downhill, and the *raths*, the fortified homesteads of Celtic Ireland, appear on the lower ground. Yet because the Irish climate is mild, it was always possible to make use of the heights and some *raths* are set high, like Caherconree in Kerry on the Slieve Mish mountains. Then too there are many small sites of the Celtic Church on the hillsides as well as the actual summit oratories on Slieve League, Croagh Patrick, Mount Brandon and Slieve Donard (36). Ireland has a cult of high places and has long cherished the old Celtic custom of lighting hilltop fires at the great seasonal changes of the year, May Day, Midsummer (St. John's Eve), Hallowe'en. Giving the old custom another twist, she has, too, of recent years erected many crosses upon the hilltops to commemorate the Church's Holy Years and the Marian Year of 1954. These crosses not only show forth the people's faith and stand as a symbol saining the fields below, but have the quite incidental value to the climber of giving him a pinpoint of the summit in mist.

The separated groups of mountains round the coast have never provided barriers, as did the Scottish and Welsh hills; their influence on Irish history has been more subtle. The great communication lines and the great barriers of Ireland are the rivers and their fords, the bogs and dry esker ridges of glacial gravels that make dry roads across them. The hillsides were the cradle of Irish farming, and the first movement of the Irish settlement pattern was downhill, to lay hold upon the riches of the plains. The plains were rich, and the immediate objective of the Anglo-Norman invaders and their successors. Cromwell's plantations gave the old inhabitants of the rich lands the choice of "hell or Connacht"—the wild moorlands and bare rocks of the west.

Forced out by the succesive plantations and seizures of the good land, the Irish retreated back into the mountains. Among the hills, on the poor land that the invader despised, the language, the culture, the religion, the traditions, were kept alive. Here the modern folklore student has gained his richest harvest, old methods still suited to the small stony fields, old traditions, old customs. With the big increase in population just before the famine of the mid-nineteenth century, the people utilised every available inch of land, and the fields climbed almost to the mountain-tops, their walls still stand. The climber will remember the evictions of the Scottish Highlands as he comes on abandoned fields and ruined cottages on the heights of the Irish hills. But these tell a different story. In Scotland the

3 Caher, Carrauntual and Beenkeragh in winter

4 Beenkeragh, Carrauntual and Caher in early spring

5 Curraghs on Inisheer with the Maumturks in the distance

6 Coumshingaun in the Comeragh mountains

hillsides were the people's rightful home, here they had always lived, and here they were turned out to give place to sheep walk and deer forest. But in Ireland, these high fields are rather the symbols of a last-ditch stand, of the ultimate retreat, the toe-hold of the Irish against the invader; from which in the end they advanced again to take possession of the soft fertility of the lowland plains. The present pattern is of the dividing up of the big lowland estates and the moving down on to them of the people from the small congested holdings of the mountainsides.

And the mountains too have been places of temporary retreat and hiding. Not only of outlaws like the famous highwayman, Crotty, with his cave in the Comeraghs, but of Irish patriots of all periods of her history. So the 1798 rising was closely linked with the Wicklow hills, in whose depths its forces were able to conceal themselves. The Irish historian, Father Geoffrey Keating, lived concealed for years in the Glen of Aherlow below the Galtees. And the constant occurrence of the word *aifrionn*, the Mass (from the Latin, *offerendum*) in place-names like Knockanaffrin (Mountain of the Mass) in the Comeraghs, reminds how the Catholic faith was kept alive during the long period of penal legislation by the courage of the priests who brought the Mass to the lonely Mass rocks on the hills and in the glens, where the people gathered, with sentries posted on the heights around them. In Donegal the cairns are still to be seen which the Catholic priests built as guides over the lonely mountain routes, each little heap set on the skyline of a ridge and in sight of the next.

Some of the mountain chains, like the Comeraghs and the Galtees, rise suddenly and abruptly from the fertile lowlands. They have virtually no foothill country at all. But others, in Kerry and Connemara and Donegal, rise from rough "mountainy" country, and it is there that one may best experience the old ways of life and hear the language spoken by the people. Here is to be seen a network of small fields, often still worked in lazy bed-ridges with the spade, for they are too small and stony for the plough. Some of these fields are, in their basic pattern, very old, for excavations at Cush on Slieve Reagh near the Galtees discovered a site dating back to the late Bronze Age whose fields still roughly corresponded to the modern ones superimposed on them. The checkerboard pattern of squarish fields, then, is very old and is connected with hand-digging and cross-ploughing with light ploughs. The English mouldboard plough, turning the soil once efficiently, imposes a characteristic long furrow to minimise turning and a rectangular field. Yet a great deal of the Irish field system is only as old as the enclosures of the late eighteenth or nineteenth century. From the air or from the mountain it is a characteristic of the country; scattered farms amongst a variegated chessboard of fields, green pasture, brown ploughland or later yellow corn, the vivid green tops of potatoes or sugar beet.

The oldest sort of settlement seems to be the *clachan*, which, like similar groupings in the Scottish Highlands, formed a small community amongst which the land was divided in rundale (or runrig) plots—each family having a turn of the different plots in sequence, so that all had a share of the use of both the best and worst land. Normally there was much mutual help and the system seems to have worked well enough, though it meant that, since one never held any particular plot permanently, there was no incentive to undertake specialised improvements, and as the cattle had the run of all the arable in winter, there was no possibility of growing special crops in winter.

Cattle from the earliest times have been the basis of the wealth of Irish farming. Sheep became important in the early nineteenth century and often replaced cattle on the hills. Sheep were kept in Celtic Ireland but only in small numbers as compared to the big herds of cattle which were maintainted by the owners of the *raths*. Great use was made of the mountain pastures, and when the cultivated land round the homesteads was sown and the crops were growing, the cattle were taken away to the high pastures. This not only meant that they were prevented from destroying the crops but also enabled a larger head of cattle to be carried. In Ireland the word for this custom of going to the mountains with cattle for the summer is "booleying". It is from the Irish word *buaile*, a cattle fold, and with a basic meaning of an enclosure. In Scotland the same custom was observed but *buaile* is rare in place-names, and the Scots called their mountain pastures and their huts "shielings". In Ireland the custom still just survives in Achill Island, and, to a rather larger extent, it is also found in Scotland, on the Hebridean island of Lewis.

So the Irish hills are marked with green plots with rickles of stone on them; the old booley sites where the people lived up in the hills herding the cattle (and wolves long remained in numbers in Ireland) and making butter from the milk. Many are the stories and traditions of the *buaile* and of the pleasant summer life amongst the mountains. Often peat (turf) for the winter firing would be cut at the same time from the mountain peat bogs. The butter was packed in wooden containers and buried in the bogs to preserve it; lost kegs are occasionally dug up today—the so-called "bog butter". Booleying went on until the sheep took over the high pastures.

Lower down, amongst the little fields, the discerning will look at the old cottages of the smallholdings. The Irish house is essentially of one basic design, rectangular, long, one room broad, and one storey high. There are two great types of this basic house: one which has a central hearth (perhaps from the old circular hut or beehive cell) and the other with the fire at the gable end. The central hearth, originally on the floor, has developed a proper chimney and therefore a dividing wall; so, too, the second type may have another room extended beyond the chimney gable, so the two designs come to approximate near to one another. Each area has its own types of thatch material and thatching method. Gabled houses are the type chiefly found in most of Ulster and Connacht and the coastal districts of Clare, Kerry and West Cork; whilst to the south of this NE.–SW. division of the country, in most of Munster and in Leinster, there are many hip-roofed houses, in which the gable is replaced by the thatch sweeping round the end of the house in a graceful half-beehive shape. The windswept west likes to secure the thatching itself with ropes and nets, and the materials used vary about the country. The climber coming down from the hills will note the long whitewashed cottages of Donegal, the beautiful hip roofs under the Knockmealdowns, the Connemara thatch roped down against the wind; and going inside the house will then discover further regional variations in the furnishings. The wet Irish climate, with a natural emphasis on the growing of oats, has helped to preserve the open fireplace and the cooking of thin cakes or oatbread on the girdle or a flagstone set before the fire. An iron crane supports the large black pot for boiling potatoes over the blaze, its ancestry going back to the archæologist's finds of similar pots of riveted metal plates, and to the gigantic pots of Irish legend.

And it is round the fire, with pot and kettle hanging from the crane, that the family and their guests sit. The table is alongside the wall, and one turns to it only if the tea is set out neatly on it; the *focus* of the Irish cottage home is the fire, not the kitchen table as in an English house of the same sort.

But the sea is not very far from the hills and, especially in the west, the small farmer is fisherman as well as farmer like his Scottish crofter counterpart. And the sea too has provided wrack to fertilise the small hill fields, and is today a valuable source of income in the way of "sea rods", the seaweed stalks collected for manufacture into the new alginate products.

So often the mountainside holding runs down from the rough hill pasture to the seashore, where the boats are hauled up on the shingle. The "mountainy" man should, says the saying, be a good hunter both on land and sea, for he comes into contact with wild nature at the two ends of his farm. The lowlander lives surrounded by cultivated land, but the mountain farmer has the wild hills and the wild sea about him, and from them both he gathers crops that he never sowed: peat (turf) for fuel, hill grazing, seaweed, fish, shell sand to lime the ground.

The speech of the western hills is Irish, and the names of all the mountains were originally Irish, though they are now sometimes replaced by English ones, and the small crop of "tourist" names like Sugarloaf. For the old people, the shepherd on the heights, every rock and hollow and streamlet had its own name, each a sensitive record of some individual feature of the place or object named. Many of these have been lost, particularly in districts in which Irish has ceased to be spoken, and, of the names preserved on the maps, many are now hard to understand owing to the English surveyors' unhappy attempts to write down a language they did not understand. In some cases the map error has passed into ordinary use and led to the loss of the correct pronunciation. Some of the map spellings are laughable, as Money scalp for *Muine sceilp*, the shrubbery of the chasm, and Vinegar Hill for *fidh na gcaer* (roughly the same sound as vinegar to English ears) which means the wood of the berries!

The common name for a hill is *sliabh*, slieve in English spelling, rough ground and translated in ordinary speech as "mountain". For an Irishman to say he is going to the "mountain" means not hill-climbing, but going out to the rough grazing. He may therefore speak of going down to the mountain. High craggy tops are called "hill" in common speech, in Irish *cnoc* (Englished as knock) and *beann* (Ben, Scots-gaelic *beinn*). Scotland has a slightly different use, *cnoc* being mainly applied to the low hillocks, *beinn* to the great heights and *sliabh* hardly occurring at all; whilst the Scottish highlander talks of going "to the hill" and not to the "mountain" to look at his sheep.

So these Irish hills are intimate with history and with men. To climb them never means wandering very far from the hillside cottages or the rough lanes (*boreens*), hung with fuchsias, that serve them. Even the main roads often climb over the mountains in a way that one never experiences, say in Scotland, and make possible a kind of armchair mountaineering. Yet there is real rock climbing to be had on many Irish cliffs and crags, though the summits may all be gained by the ordinary hill walker. And storm and snow and cold can strike as fiercely on their heights as in countries regarded as more strictly mountainous. And then, too, it is perhaps in the hills that the beginning of the understanding of the whole country can be made, to look down upon the plains and upon the sea from the silence of the high places, and to begin to know the Irish people in the intimacy of the semicircle round the open fire.

CHAPTER II

Connemara

EACH mountain district in Ireland has its own distinctive flavour, its own individuality, but nowhere is that flavour so varied or individuality so distinct as amongst the mountains of Connemara and South Mayo, the miniature alps that rise in a fantastic pattern of crag and valley between Galway Bay in the south and Clew Bay in the north.

It seems almost that in this country all the possible sorts of mountain scenery are represented. There is the solitary cone of Croagh Patrick (8), the rock ridges and precipices of the Twelve Bens (11) and the Maumturks (10), the red sandstone crags and corries of Mweelrea (13) and Ben Gorm, the down-like swards of the Sheeffry hills, the high level peat hags of the Partry mountains. Corrie lakes are cradled under their summits, the fiord of Killary Harbour twists inland from the Atlantic, reflecting the steep mountain slopes in its still, salt water (12); deep glens snake between the ranges with sparkling lakes nestling on their floors, streams fall from the heights in cataracts, and all the while the background is the sea, the hard horizon line of the Atlantic and the scattered green shapes of the offshore islands, the waves breaking on dazzlingly white beaches.

You may see this country from the Aran Islands as a line of shapely heights, across whose tops hail showers stalk whilst Galway Bay basks in the sun; or you may see the same mountains from the white limestone ridges of Clare with the blue of Galway Bay between you and them and the flanks of the Twelve Bens all dappled with cloud shadows. Or you may stand on the top of the tower of Ross Errily Abbey and look across Corrib Lough to the Maumturks and the Partrys, high upland, a wall of rock springing up from the Irish plains. Or yet again, see Croagh Patrick lift like the Matterhorn from Clew Bay shore as you come down the Westport road from Castlebar.

7 The Connemara mountains. Glen Inagh, with the Twelve Bens, Mweelrea and the Maumturk mountains

8 Croagh Patrick and the pilgrim path to the summit chapel

9 The Glen of the Downs and the Great Sugar Loaf, Co. Wicklow

CONNEMARA

But from wherever you look at it, the shape and pattern of the picture depends on two things, the mountain and the sea. Connemara life is never very far from either of them; either you come up against the mountains or down to the beach where the clear sea curls in angry breakers on the rocks or the long beach. And it is in the coastal strip between hill and sea that the little farms are concentrated: two-thirds of this wild land of West Connacht has never been cultivated. And so the beauty of this mountainous shoulder of Ireland that juts out into the Atlantic is the mingled beauty of hill and shore and island; and just because of that fact, the colours are hard and sharp and clear, a blue and vivid sea whose deeps are peacock and whose shallows emerald, mudless, for the rivers run short and fast from the hills, tinged only with the tawny brew of the peat bogs, and with white sand beaches backed by pale green grass on dunes, the flare of fuchsia hedges, the dazzle of daisies on the little seaside fields, the glitter and glisten of the sunshine on the wet quartzites of the Twelve Bens. Connemara, the sunlight filtered and softened by the moisture in the air (Delphi Lodge under Mweelrea has recorded 99 inches of rain in the year), is a land of softly blue skies, a blue that seems reflected, crystallised, in the blue of the sheep's bit clinging to the grey rock of the mountains and the lone tufts of harebells on the Maumturk heights, a country of sudden sunshine after rain, lighting green islets rising from a shimmering sea, dappled and wind-rippled like watered silk. It is a country where the low sun of the very early morning strikes the quartzites of the Twelve Bens and shows them in sudden relief, with a faint flush of pink, themselves reflected in the mirror-smooth lake below. It is a country where the dawn may come up over snow-covered heights and tinge them vividly red, or where the autumn sun may gleam out after rain and show all the moorland a rich golden brown, marked with the dark blots of peat cutting and peat stack. This fervour of colour, a colour that is both bright and yet softened and filtered by the moist air, is as much a part of the Connemara scene as the panniered donkeys coming into market with cabbage and herrings and mackerel and carrots, or the curraghs out fishing for pollock, or the brown shawl on the woman with the red skirt at the holy well on Pattern (the patron saint's) Day.

THE MOUNTAINS OF IRELAND

The mountains begin in the north, around Clew Bay, with the dramatic challenge of Croagh Patrick, the lone hill that is Ireland's holy mountain and St. Patrick's choice of a desert retreat (8). Out to sea the stumpy hill of Clare Island takes up the challenge in a kind of half-formed imitation, Croagh Patrick without the summit, a broken tooth. North, across the bay, the heights of Achill spring up in steep cones of hard quartzite and east of them are the flowing upland shapes of the Nephin mountains. South from Croagh Patrick begin the real mountain ranges of Connemara, the grassy high-level plateau of the Sheeffry hills, facing Croagh Patrick, and separated by a deep and narrow glen from the red sandstone crags and corries of the Ben Gorm group. South, the fiord of Killary cuts deep into the land and a valley leads north from its shores between the Sheeffrys and the Mweelrea group, whose summit at 2688 feet, broods over the mouth of Killary Harbour and is the highest land in Connemara (13). The salt water, snaking amongst the mountains, ends at Aasleagh, where the river plunges into it in waterfalls, but the hollow itself continues northward toward Westport, with the ridges of Ben Gorm upon the one hand and the haggy tableland of the Partry mountains on the other. Beyond the Partrys are the great inland lakes of Mask and Corrib, the later forming a waterway to Galway town. From the head of Killary, too, there is another through valley that goes south to Corrib between the Partry and Devil's Mother group and the long rock ridge of the Maumturks (10). Across the Maumturks, to the west, is the parallel north–south valley of Glen Inagh, and on its farther, western side, the compact group of quartzite mountains that go by the name of the Twelve Bens and form a kind of miniature mountainland all on their own, little mountains with real and severe rock-climbs on the flanks of their bleak ridges. Finally, as a kind of trimming, there is a circle of little coastal hills: Errisbeg above Roundstone forming a lone hump in the waste of Connemara bogland, Tully facing out to Inishbofin, and the mountain massif of Doughruagh behind Kylemore.

But whilst each group is different in its own individual character and nature, the outlook from them all is essentially the same, varying only with the position and angle from which it is seen. It is always the mountain round one and the sea at its feet, a sea whose islands vary from the spire-like summits of Achill to the low tableland of the green and holy island of Caher. Distantly across Galway Bay are the white limestones of the Burren hills in County Clare; distantly across Clew Bay, the rolling heathery uplands of the Nephin mountains. And when the weather is particularly clear, far away, almost like a mirage, the line of Mount Brandon and the Killarney mountains rise in the south, with a line of cumulus above the ragged summit line.

It is with the 2688 feet of Mweelrea (*An Maol riabhach*, the grey or brindled bald mountain) that one should perhaps begin and at the very start see it from the seaside and from below. It rises at the mouth of Killary (*Caol sháile*, the narrow sea inlet) fiord, in a single magnificent upsweep from the sand and dunes of the shore, through the small farms of the coast and on up to the rocky crown that forms the summit(7). The western gales strike against this great face of mountain, and in winter the snow clings in a corniced ruff along its summit; over it the clouds gather in storm, or in clearing weather lift off it into massive piles of cumulus. And from it you may look down upon all the mountain and sea of Connemara.

Inland the mountain forms a horseshoe ridge, one steep flank above the fiord, marked with deserted houses and old fields along the shore, the other curving round about Doo Lough to Delphi Lodge and the valley across which rises Ben Gorm and the Sheeffry hills. It is from Fin Lough on the little road from Killary Harbour to Doo Lough that one may conveniently begin the climb. (Doo Lough is *Dubh loch*, the black lake, Fin is *finn*, white. I follow the ordnance map spellings for convenience, *lough* should correctly be *loch* as in Scotland—the *gh* is the English attempt to write the guttural *ch*.)

I went up Mweelrea one March morning in bright sunshine, up the long slope from the road below, a slope of boggy grass littered with rocks, which brings one suddenly upon the lip of the precipitous rocks overlooking Doo Lough, one of those ascents on which the view flashes out suddenly before one as the last few feet are mounted. So, standing amongst the violet sandstone rocks, I looked down upon Clew Bay, a delicate blue, the summit of Croagh Patrick, wet with melted hoar frost and flashing like silver in the sun, the cliffs of Achill, and the cloud-dapples on the slopes of the Nephins; whilst immediately at hand were the mountains and on the level at their feet, around Louisburgh, the little fields and white cottages. The way continues on above Doo Lough, keeping along the craggy edge of the great corrie wall above it, gritty red sandstone with jasper and other pebbles in conglomerate bands. In the morning light the corrie itself was a violet hazed bowl with Glencullin Lough (a smaller lake above Doo Lough) lying at its foot and coloured a deep indigo-blue.

The ridge turns away towards the west and a col before the final rise, a broader and more grassy shoulder, to the summit of Mweelrea. The outlook broadens to include the islands and the sandy strand and the fiord inlet of Killary. Upon the col itself are stony boulder beds with the faint trace of rough buildings constructed from them, likely enough booley huts to make use of the short Mweelrea turf. Up here, one may well recall Roderick O'Flaherty's account of West Connacht in 1684:

> The country is generally coarse, moorish and mountainous, full of high rocky hills, large valleys, great bogs, some woods, whereof it had abundance before they were cut.

And of the booley, he wrote:

> In summer time they (the inhabitants) drive their cattle to the mountains, where such as look to the cattle live in small cabbins for that season.

From the summit itself, a shorter and steeper ridge descends along the side of Killary Harbour, from which one may look into the southern corries of Mweelrea, cradled under the peak itself, backed by mural walls of sandstone and holding a shallow lochan, boulder strewn, with a yellow delta of sand at its mouth.

Mweelrea, the Sheeffry hills and Ben Gorm (*gorm*, blue or green) are of much later date geologically than the pre-Cambrian quartzite heights across the Killary depression which build the Twelve Bens and the Maumturks. Mweelrea and Ben Gorm are sandstone and conglomerate, the softer contours of the Sheeffrys are based on shale and flagstone (these rocks, and those of the Partry mountains, are of Ordovician and Silurian Age). The deep glen that leads from that in which Doo Lough lies, up between the Sheeffry hills and Ben Gorm, with a pleasant little road along the floor of it, is a good starting-point from which to gain either of these two ridges. The highest point of the Sheeffry hills is 2504 feet; it is a broad and undulating upland ridge, with crags here and there upon the north side, looking across to Croagh Patrick. The view is one that seems to range the very ends of the earth, from the islands alternately lit by the sun or blotted out by passing storms, to the blue-hazed distance of the inland plains of Ireland. The sheep graze to the summits and there in August I met shepherds gathering the flock for a dipping: "It's not often you meet a woman here," said one of them.

Ben Gorm across the glen has splendid crags of sandstone, frequented by nimble goats, and even more splendid views of Mweelrea and the Twelve Bens. It rises to 2303 feet. The top above the glen between is the craggy mountain, Ben Creggan, and this leads on and up to Ben Gorm. It has all the delights of sandstone mountains, the scattered boulders with a multitude of different shapes, the tufts of blaeberries and clustered St. Patrick's cabbage, and ferns in the rock clefts. The waterfalls that descend the Sheeffry slope opposite roar in one's ears as one climbs up. Like Mweelrea, there is a horseshoe circuit to be made of the crags from the east, ascending by the ridge of Ben Creggan and descending by that of Ben Gorm, from which one looks down on that silent and mysterious head of Killary Harbour and the pine-fringed waterfall of Aasleagh.

From these mountains you can see the bedding and folding of the sandstones set out upon the hillsides, like a diagram, and follow the line of the softer shales in the hollows of the hills. Yet the climber will almost instinctively turn away from these heights to the lower but more adventurous rocks of the Twelve Bens.

These bare hills are quartzite, part of the pre-Cambrian complex of Connemara, its hardest part standing up from the planed levels at their foot of more readily eroded rocks— granite and schist and Connemara marble. The Twelve Bens, the *Beanna Beola* (11), radiate from a central height and a central gap in starfish fashion, rocky ridges lifting from boggy glens and showing from the distance a skyline broken by a series of tops which can be conveniently called (if not actually numbered off) Twelve. So O'Flaherty says: "The twelve high mountains of Bennabeola, called by mariners the twelve stakes, being the first land they discover as they come from the maine." Correctly they should be called the Beanna Beola, Beola's mountains, Beola being a mythical personage said by tradition to be buried on the lowland of Connemara by the sea at Toombeola, Beola's burial mound.

Like the Maumturks across Glen Inagh, the Twelve Bens are real rock mountains, to be treated with respect and presenting the rock-climber with sport on their cliff faces. They are bare and hard and slippery, intensely ice moulded, white, grey or pink quartzite, here and there patterned with violet lichens. The hill walker should remember that the ridges are cliff bound and that he cannot get off them just where he chooses if the weather breaks when he is traversing them. Not all the ridges present the same rockiness or their cliffs the same degree of difficulty; the most exciting is the line above Glen Inagh, from the gap under Ben Baun to Derryclare.

These mountains were, at one stage of the Ice Age, a centre of ice formation and dispersion. It has been estimated that at one phase this ice lay to a depth of 2000 feet and formed a part of the general ice sheet covering Ireland, the Connemara hills being one source of the ice. The icefloes pushed out from this centre, eroding the Killary inlet into a fiord, spreading north into Mayo and west through Clew Bay, south-east to Galway, the track of the ice movement into the Central Plain blazed by dropped boulders of recognisable Galway granite. At another period there were local glaciations, so that the climber not only walks the smooth ice rounded ridges, but sees the corries plucked out in the crags below and the morainic ridges of sand and gravel deposited by the melt waters from the foot of local glaciers in the hill glens.

The central and highest point of the Beanna Beola is the white Ben Baun (*Beann bán*, the white mountain, 2395 feet). To the northward, a col leads to the ridge of Ben Brack (*Beann breac*, the speckled mountain) above the glen of Kylemore (*An choill mhor*, the great wood) with its chain of lakes; while to the west is the undulating ridgewalk of Muckanaght (*Muiceannach*, place frequented by pigs) and Bencullagh (peak of the grouse). South from Ben Baun the rocks fall steeply to the central pass through the range which provides a cross-country walk from the head-waters of the Owenglin River into Glen Inagh. Beyond this rocky gap they rise yet more steeply to the two southern ridges of the group, of Ben Corr (*Beann Corr*, peak of the conical hill) and Derryclare, and of Ben Breen (*Beann Bruighin*, peak of the hostel) and Ben Gower (*Beann-gabher*, mountain of goats).

From the level moors of the through valley of Glen Inagh, with its island-dotted lake, one looks up to the Maumturks upon the one hand, which have been described as the Twelve Bens arranged in line instead of clustered in a group, and on the other to the Derryclare ridge and to Ben Baun. Looking up to it from the valley, this ridge appears a knife-edge of bare rock, grey, white, tinged with pink, changing with the light and shadow, an invitation and a challenge. In the south, between Derryclare Lough and Lough Inagh, Derryclare Mountain (*Doirín clár*, wood of the plain, 2220 feet) sends down a long bare rocky spur to the valley, up which one may walk, the way becoming steadily rockier and wilder. From thence, enclosing rock-bound corrie hollows, the cliff leads in a wild line to Ben Corr (2336 feet) and to Bencollaghduff (mountain of the black boar, 2290 feet), from which the rocks fall sheerly to the central gap. These two heights north of Derryclare send shorter and more precipitous spurs out to Glen Inagh. From the corries between these spurs the streams run crystal clear from the bare rocks down into the peat bogs, the pebbles sparkling through the shimmering water.

Yet in fact the knife-edge of the valley view is an illusion, and when you come out upon the crest of Derryclare you walk on along a broad and rocky back rather than a sharp ridge. Its ups and downs, however, are craggy and steep and the route needs selection; it is a scramble rather than a walk in several places. But even here I saw the remains of an old building, probably a booley, and found the sheep nibbling the bites of heather and grass amongst the waste of rock. Mostly it is bare rock and littered boulders and screes, with club mosses and dwarf junipers—devoid of water except for stagnant pools of rain in the hollows; a thirsty place on a hot summer day. Below, in one of the small hillside cottages, a man told me how he had tried to quench a thirst up on these rocks by squeezing the damp from the bog moss, a tale, perhaps, but with the truth of the nature of these ridges in it.

The angle of the outlook changes from these Twelve Bens. From Mweelrea and Ben Gorm it was of mountains, sea and islands; now one looks directly down upon the great level bogland, all silver threaded with lake and stream that makes up southern Connemara, a flat bog broken by sudden rises like the hill of Cashel (1024 feet) and Errisbeg (987 feet). Beyond this strange wet country's deeply indented coastline is the broad spread of Galway Bay. The great level, from which the quartzite hills rise so dramatically and sharply, is one of the several "peneplain" levels of Ireland. During the sculpturing of the present land-surface in the geological past, the land has stood at varying levels and the long processes of weathering produced a general levelling, a peneplain. Later uplifts meant that these old erosion surfaces were elevated and the rivers began to cut down through them again: at least four such levels are known in Ireland, two high on the mountain-tops, one about 600 feet, and the lowest forming the great Central Plain and the main lowland of Ireland. The passage of the ice sheets over this Connemara lowland produced the hollows in which the lakes now lie, in the proportion of about one of water to thirty-three parts of land.

This country of moor and lake is perhaps even better seen from the southern ridge of the Twelve Bens, of Ben Breen (2276 feet), Ben Gower (2184 feet) and Benlettery (*Beann leitirigh*, the mountain of the wet hillside, 1904 feet). Ascending from the gap below Ben Baun, the rocks of Ben Breen are slabby, like the tiles of the roof of Ireland. The outlook is perhaps the best to be got from the Bens, for you are out on the western snout of the group, with the whole coastline of the west below you. So the eye ranges from Ben Baun close at hand, its quartzite flashing white in the sunshine, and from the grey cliffs and grassy slopes round one, across to Mweelrea and the Sheeffrys, through the gaps of the Maumturk passes to Lough Corrib, through the Sheeffry passes to Croagh Patrick; and then the whole range of the Irish coast from Achill and Clare Island, down by Inishbofin and Inishark to the Aran Islands, and on to the Clare hills and the cliffs of Moher. Beyond them, most distantly, with still cumulus hanging above them, the shadowy line of the Killarney Reeks and Mount Brandon and the Blasket Islands. The sea changes with the light, blue to the north, as I saw it one September day, and a silver mirror reflecting the cloud shapes to the south. Immediately below are the boglands and the white coralline strands of Connemara: inlet, island, cliff and shore.

10 The Maumturks, Co. Galway

11 The Twelve Bens, Co. Galway

12 Killary Harbour, Ireland's only fiord, Co. Mayo

13 Mweelrea (2,688 feet), Co. Mayo

THE TWELVE BENS

The islands themselves are a litany of the Celtic saints, from Caher of St. Patrick to Aran of St. Enda, from Ard Oilen (high island) of St. Fechin and St. MacDara's Island of Sinach MacDara. To sail out to these islands is to look back to the whole line of the Connemara hills and that is perhaps the most impressive view of the mountains of all, the silvery Bens slashed by their central gap, Mweelrea's steep flank and the cone of Croagh Patrick to the north.

Yet this is but a taste of the attraction of the Twelve Bens. There are those many delightful lesser heights and ridges, the solitary silver cone of the Diamond above Kylemore and the enchanting easy ridgewalk of Ben Brack looking down upon the lakes and rhododendrons of Kylemore. There are the rocks of Doughruagh across that Kylemore glen, and hidden beyond it the unexpectedly fertile oasis of Salruck, wooded and sheltered and once a place of pilgrimages in honour of a saint called Roc, of whom nothing seems certainly known. There is a solitary grass-grown track from Salruck round the shores of Killary Harbour to Leenane at its head. There are the surprising red and green flags of the roadside outcrops near Lough Fee (*Loch Fidh*, lake of the wood), stone walls and buildings technicolored with them. There are the thick fuchsia hedges of the roadsides, orange in early spring when the sap begins to run, fires of red blossom later on. There are the great clumps of royal fern in the bogs, uncurling golden yellow fronds in spring. There is the blue sheep's bit of the lower rocks, the brilliance of the tall gorse in spring ("English" gorse) and of the dwarf gorse ("Welsh" gorse) in autumn. The moorlands about Roundstone have, in late summer, a kind of Turkish carpet spread over them of brilliant bell heather mingled with the yellow cushions of the dwarf gorse. Incidently, gorse is the English name for the bushes; the Irish always call it furze and the Scots, whins. Often, as at the holy well of Kilgeever under Croagh Patrick, the dwarf gorse forms round clumps interwoven with heather, a most splendid sight of yellow blossom mingled with the pinks and reds of bell heather, ling and St. Dabeoc's heath.

The lowland between sea and mountain, with its small hills, presents a constantly changing variation of the basic Connemara theme of sea and hill, of the pattern of small stone-walled fields and whitewashed cottages. And always the mountains in the background, whether you watch the horse races on the vast strand of Omey or go out to the islands.

The Maumturk mountains, east of Glen Inagh (*Gleann eidhnach*, glen of ivy), are a long line of naked rock, zigzagging from north to south, and cut by two principal passes, both old cross-country routes and both with a holy well marking their summit. From these passes the range gets its name, for Maum is *Mám*, a mountain pass. The second syllable is *torc*, the wild boar. Actually, one pass of the range seems to have been named the boar's pass, Maumturk, and then this name given to the whole group. The northern pass across the range has a holy well dedicated to St. Fechin of Fore and an excellent spring; that to the south in Maumeen is St. Patrick's, still, unlike St. Fechin's, occasionally visited, but once the venue of an enormous gathering. It cured not only men but beasts as well, and the cure began as soon as the messenger had set off to bring water back from the blessed spring.

Like the Twelve Bens, the Maumturks offer serious hill-climbing with real cliffs. Down these descend some fine waterfalls, and in mist, in Glen Inagh below, I have seen the waterfall without the rock behind it being visible, a ribbon hanging in space like the grin of the Cheshire cat. The highest point of the ridge is 2307 feet. It is one of the big expeditions of Irish hill-walking to traverse the complete line of Maumturks, from the subsidiary outpost of Leckavrea Mountain (*Leac aimhreidh*, rough flagstones, 2174 feet) above Maam Cross, over Maumeen Pass (*Máimín*, little pass), along the main ridge and eventually down to Leenane at the head of Killary. The famous climber and botanist, H. C. Hart, is said to have taken fourteen hours on this ridgewalk. But the traverse of the main and highest part of the ridge, from St. Fechin's Well to St. Patrick's, is easily within a day's compass.

I took that route in August, going up from the east flank of the mountains at Bealanabrack, where the cottage gardens had bushes of vividly blue hydrangeas in flower. The glen has a boggy floor and grassy flanks, along it are ruined cottages and the walls of an old fort. A trace of a track leads up to St. Fechin's Well, a tremendous view down to the pass of Kylemore and the sea beyond, and from there a scramble takes one on to the rocks of the ridge. Rock and more rock is the pattern, schist at first, then grey quartzite with pink tinted patches and pale green stripes and jewelled with little clumps of blue harebells, with tuffets of bell and ling heather and of thrift. Again, that outlook to sea and mountain, but with the variation that the parallel rocks of the Twelve Bens across Glen Inagh dominate the immediate scene. And on the other hand, there is the great inland lake of Lough Corrib, with its islands, the most of which is masked by these same Maumturks in the outlook from the other mountains.

The ridge zigzags, and there is a descent and then a steep climb up to the highest point; scrambling up about a thousand feet over screes which look vertical but are not, and then over ridge upon ridge of rock. From the big summit cairn one walks round a corrie which has fluted cliffs of quartzite and two little castellated turrets of rock to decorate it. There is a second corrie, another descent and a final pull up over more screes to the last height above Maumeen and the descent to the old cross-country track. Roseroot grows in the rocks above that pass, and the Leckavrea slopes, below the cliffs across the valley, are purpled with heather.

Parallel to Glen Inagh, dividing the Maumturks from the mountains farther east, is the deep glen that leads from Leenane to Maam Cross. East of it you are off the quartzites, and the mountains rise in gentler and grassier uplands. Hidden amongst them is the lake of Lough Nafooey (*Loch na feothaidh*, or perhaps *na fuaithe*, lake of hate). The Partry mountains (named from the people who inhabited that country, the Partraighe) form a plateau whose summit is a wasteland of peat hags. Its highest point is Maumtrasna (transverse pass, 2239 feet). The best feature of this massive tableland is its rim, eaten out into fine corries holding lakes. Then, above Leenane on Killary, is the isolated and grassy Devil's Mother (2131 feet) which provides a commanding outlook surveying all this land of bog and grassy slope and crag. It is quickly climbed from Leenane, leaving behind in the valley the small houses and small fields, in autumn with the stacks of turf (peat) and hay all neatly thatched and corded down against the weather—with, in some cases, home-made ropes of twisted grass and rush.

From the summit of the Devil's Mother, the pilgrim path up Croagh Patrick shows as a white ribbon up the mountain, and below one is the main road from Clifden to Westport, traversing the floor of the deep glen between the Partry mountains and Ben Gorm. Just before this road leads into Westport, the town at the head of Clew Bay, one can turn off along the Louisburgh road for the start of the pilgrim path up St. Patrick's Mountain or, better still, turn off farther south along a small trackway that leads to a quicker and easier scramble up the southern flank of the mountain.

Croagh Patrick (2510 feet) is the most climbed mountain in Ireland, but it is not mountaineers that do the climbing but the ordinary folk who normally set no feet on hill ground. Here St. Patrick spent a whole Lent in prayer and penance for the people of Ireland, and here each year, on the last Sunday of July, the Irish come in their thousands (the last few years have seen pilgrimages estimated at fifty to sixty thousand) by special bus and train, by car, on foot, on cycle, to climb the hill, say the traditional stational prayers, hear Mass and receive Communion on the summit.

I have been on Croagh Patrick for that mighty gathering of the nation, standing through the short summer night on the bare rock of the conical summit, with shadowy figures and murmured prayers surging round me, and I have climbed there alone in springtime and in summer. Yet perhaps I like Croagh Patrick best in winter, under snow, the solitary hill flashing white in the sunshine. I went up one February day when there were patches of ice on the roads below and snow on the tops, a day to be snatched at, for the snow does not normally lie long in Connemara. The willows by the lowland road were orange-twigged with running sap, the world was stirring with spring, but the cone of Croagh Patrick above was brilliantly whitened with snow.

Perched upon the southern shore of Clew Bay, this isolated mountain looks on the one hand to the mountains of Connemara and to the other across Clew Bay, to the Nephin mountains of North Mayo. At Clew Bay, the Central Plain reaches the western sea, and the islands of the bay are partly submerged drumlins, the whaleback ridges of rock and gravel moulded by the passage of the ice over the low country. So from Croagh Patrick one looks not only to mountains but into the vast blue distances of the level plain to the east. This particular day the Nephin mountains were snow-covered and reflected in the still sea below them. The lower slopes of Croagh Patrick were merely frozen, but, as I gained the ridge, I found great wreaths of crisp granular snow lying across the pilgrim path. Ahead, the final cone rose white and immaculate. The bay itself was violet blue, the moors olive, the snow flashed against a vivid blue sky. I kicked steps up the ascent, of smooth steep unblemished snow, and came eventually upon the crest, with the small concrete Mass chapel all furred in ice and the cross on its gable displaying long streamers of sparkling ice.

The wind had swept the actual summit clear of snow, but hung these icy streamers on chapel and the posts that support the temporary bothies that sell refreshments to the pilgrims. The ground was starred with flowers of ice. There was an odd sense of being poised between earth and sky, between the brown moors below and the blue sky above.

From Croagh Patrick one looks to North Mayo, the undulating lonely uplands of the Nephin Beg mountains (2369 feet at their highest) and to the solitary hump of Nephin (*Cnoc Neifinn*, 2646 feet) to the east of them. About that whole country between Clew Bay and Killala Bay to the north is a sense of space and desolation, of broad shoulders of remote mountains rising from a great desert land of level bog across which the roads run white and solitary. Not perhaps so deserted now, for these great bogs are being commercially exploited for the winning of turf (peat) and are gay with the bright paint of the new Irish machinery for its mechanical digging. Around the rim of this wasteland, on the sandy dune land of the Mullet, or on the little islands of Inishglora of St. Brendan and of Duvillaun, are many sites of early Irish life, cliff fort and church and old traditions of the saints.

Achill Island, now reached by a road-bridge, with its tremendous cliffs and rocky heights, provides some attractive climbing. Here too is the last station of active booleying in Ireland. Its name is *Acaill*, said to be derived from the word for an eagle, and recalling that eagles were once common on the Irish mountains, their presence there still remembered in place-names. The golden eagle has been gone from Ireland for less than a hundred years—it is said to have been seen about Achill at the beginning of the present century, and the white-tailed sea-eagle to have been still abundant there in 1838: also that Achill was without foxes until the bridge across the sound linking the island with the mainland was built.

Nephin has upon its summit some much ruined and pulled about prehistoric cairns. Their name is Leacht Fhinn, the cairn of Finn or Fionn, and it seems that this lonely top is one of the several places which tradition ascribes as a burial-place of the hero. The mountain itself standing alone, distinct from the main mass of North Mayo hills, is both a great landmark in the west of Ireland and a great view-point. From it one may in clear weather see north up to the Donegal mountains.

At the hill-foot, where the bogland merges into dryer, greener pasture, the low-lying meadows are sheeted with orchids in summertime. The mountain itself is heathery, with the rock breaking through here and there; as you ascend the heather grows progressively shorter and finally gives place to moss and blaeberry and tufts of thrift. Lough Conn (*Loch con*, hound's lake) lies immediately below to the east, rimmed by a checker-board pattern of small fields.

This is Mayo, not Connemara. It is more desolate, more spacious, wilder, less inhabited. The Mediterranean heath is in flower on the slopes of the Nephins in spring and from Mallaranny one looks through a frame of fuchsias to Croagh Patrick, but the countryside is hardening in tone, this brown bogland and dark moor is a fitting intermediary between the brilliance of the colour of Connemara, with its lush fertility in its sheltered hollows, and the harsher accents and countryside of the north, of the green and grey of Ben Bulben and the trim whitewashed Donegal cottages in their setting of mountain and valley, mountains and glens of a more subdued colouring than those of Connemara.

CHAPTER III

Sligo and Donegal

DONEGAL, *Dun na nGall*, the Stronghold of the Stranger, but anciently the country of Conall, *Tír Chonaill*, the north-west corner of Ireland; is it of mountains or of men that one should write? For here is some of the most attractive terrain to the climber in Ireland, and here too is ground historic in the country's story, last to retain the old Celtic way of life, the shore from which the earls sailed in 1607 when the Irish cause seemed entirely lost, the country of the Four Masters gathering the last scraps of Irish history and tradition, and the country, too, of the great stone fort of Grianan of Aileach and of St. Columcille, perhaps Ireland's greatest son.

The way by which one should approach *Tír Chonaill* is from the south, by Sligo and Ben Bulben, so that, as the road heads north beside the sea, the Donegal mountains spring suddenly into view before one in a long line of massive hills. It is indeed possible to drive the whole length of Ireland in the day and stay in sight of the Irish mountains all the way. For if you begin in the south in Cork, the road is first in sight of the Galtees and Ballyhoura hills, and, leaving them, approaches the high ground around Limerick and about Lough Derg on the Shannon —the Slieve Felim and Slieve Aughty mountains. Between Limerick and Galway the road looks across to the bare limestone heights of the Burren, and then from the Galway–Tuam road there is a wonderful prospect across the level plain and Lough Corrib to the Connemara mountains, the Twelve Bens, Maumturks, Partrys. Beyond, still heading north for Sligo, Croagh Patrick stands sentinel in the west, and then by Tobercurry one comes in sight of the Ox mountains, the high ground between Killala and Sligo Bay, and so to the hills grouped about Sligo itself.

The Ox mountains rise to 1786 feet, and have nothing to do

with oxen. Their proper name is the stony mountains, *Sliabh ghamh*, which has been confused with *dhamh*, which would mean ox mountains.

There is a sharp contrast between these dark, heathery, and sometimes rocky hills and the green and grey of the limestone hills to the north of Sligo, and which, in point of fact, lie partly in Co. Sligo and partly in Leitrim. The Ox mountains are an offshoot of the metamorphic rocks of Connemara, and also show in their NE.–SW. trend the line of Caledonian folding that is so marked a feature of Donegal itself.

As you come down into Sligo town itself there is a round hill with an enormous round cairn on the top of it standing out away to the west. It is Knocknarea (*Cnoc*, or sometimes *Ard*, *na righadh*, the hill of the executions) and it brings one into contact with two very different things that are never far away from the climber in Ireland, the great stone cairns of hillside and hilltop, and the great Irish collections of stories about the legendary heroes of the past. Knocknarea is 1078 feet high and the cairn, the *Miscaun Meadhbh*, is said to commemorate Queen Maeve (*Meabh*, Shakespeare's Mab) of the Ulidian tales. It is an immense structure, measuring about 200 feet in diameter and undisturbed. It probably contains a passage grave, for it lies in country immensely rich in structures of this sort.

It seems probable that the Megalithic chambered cairn is developed from a burial in cave—to make an artificial cave with great stones in lieu of the natural article. There are various types of these great cairns in Ireland, falling into two main classes: the gallery grave, with a long narrow chamber in which the burials were made, and the passage grave, in which a passage leads into the burial chamber or chambers. Of this last sort are the famous tumuli of New Grange and Dowth on the Boyne, and the Sligo country is important in seeing an intermingling of the two types, the westward spread of the passage grave from the Boyne meeting the NE.–SW. development of the horned gallery graves of Ulster and Donegal.

The horned or court cairn is a special type of the gallery grave in which there was a ritual forecourt, unroofed, before the entry into the burial chamber. In the east, these horned cairns are of simpler pattern than those in the west in Sligo, Mayo and Donegal, and it is possible either that their builders came first

14 The ridge of Errigal, Co. Donegal

15 The stone fort of Grianan of Ailech in Donegal

16 Altan Lough and the Aghla More-Muckish ridge

to the Carlingford area in Ulster and moved west, developing a more complex type of tomb as they did so, or else that the reverse happened—that they came from the west and that the cairn type was simplified with time.

So round about the cairn of Maeve on Knocknarea are many important Megalithic sites. At Carrowmore, just east of Knocknarea, is a group of passage graves, numbering originally about sixty in all. At Carrowkeel, farther south in the same county, were fourteen cairns of the same kind. Deerpark, just north of Sligo town, has the ruin of a horned cairn, and another horned cairn was excavated to the north of Deerpark at Creevykeel. This Creevykeel cairn was early Bronze Age in date, but after it had become partly ruined, was made use of by a group of iron-workers in early Christian times, an interesting association in view of the legends, like that of Wayland Smith, which associate these ancient cairns with metal working.

The chambered cairn was originally covered with a great mound of smaller stones, but often is now marked merely by the denuded core of great stones which formed the burial chamber. These relics go by many names like "dolmen" and "cromlech", and often on the Irish maps, Dermot and Grania's Bed, *Leaba Dhiarmuda's Gráinne*. With Maeve and with Diarmaid (*Dermot*) we are back at the two great cycles of Irish storytelling, the Ulster cycle and the Finnian one. How far do these two great collections of stories relate to anything real at all? Prof. T. F. O'Rahilly held that both were to do with the Celtic gods and goddesses, later spoken of as though they were historic persons who had certain magical powers, that the Finn cycle was purely mythological but that the Ulster cycle had some historic material incorporated relating to the struggle between the provinces of Ulster and Connacht.

Both have left their mark in place-name and tradition. The Ulster cycle, of which the most famous tale is the *Táin Bó Cualnge*, the cattle raid of Cooley, and in which Maeve appears, is tied down to particular places in Ireland. The cycle relating to the doings of Finn and the Fiana is not so localised and can always be conveniently accommodated to the storyteller's own countryside. Hence the number of mountains called Seefin, *Suidhe Fhinn*, Finn's Seat, and the many cromlechs named from the story of the elopement of Diarmaid with Grainne. The series was equally popular in Scotland and there again it was localised over and over again. The extraordinary affair of Macpherson's *Ossian* showed that even in the eighteenth century the story, even in Macpherson's version with Finn appearing as Fingal, could still be very popular.

Was there ever a real Fiana? It seems possible that there was, that, copied from the Roman legions, the Irish did have a small commando kind of body of picked men in the period immediately before the introduction of Christianity. To this reality it would be easy to add wonder stories and mythological themes culled from the older sagas of Celtic gods. These saga themes were later on to be utilised in stories of the lives of the Celtic saints. They were good stories and the Irish liked them, and it is, I think, as stories they always regarded them rather than as history. Scientific hagiography is a modern thing: the old "Life" of a saint was meant to edify and point a moral rather than keep to the strict facts of history.

The road north out of Sligo keeps beside the sea, between the shore and the great limestone mass of Ben Bulben which dominates the whole southern end of Donegal Bay. Ben Bulben (*Beann Gulban*, Gulba's mountain, 1730 feet) forms the western end of this crag-edged plateau, facing the sea in a long narrow ridge shaped like the prow of a ship (18). Inland, the flat-topped plateau rimmed with its grey cliffs rises to its highest point in Truskmore's 2113 feet (*Trosc*, a codfish). On either side of the Ben Bulben–Truskmore mass are glens with beautiful lakes cradled on their floors, Glenade Lough in the north (*Gleann éatha*, glen of jealousy) and Glen Car in the south (*Gleann a chartha*, glen of the rock).

The main road, nosing round the prow of Bulben, comes of a sudden in sight of the whole of Donegal Bay, a vividly blue sea and beyond it the mountains and cliffs of Donegal, culminating in the almost sheer rise of nearly 2000 feet of Slieve League. This is the essence of southern Donegal: the heather and the rock of the north shore of the bay, and the grey and green of the Ben Bulben hills in the south; between them the white gold sands of Bundoran and Rosnowlagh with behind them green undulating fields, hedges felted with honeysuckle and guarded with lines of purple foxgloves.

This north-west is, in fact, for the man interested in the

mountain flowers and plants, the richest in Ireland, and the Ben Bulben cliffs carry a rich alpine flora, whilst below in the woodland of the valleys the arbutus is to be found.

Looking back to the limestone hills of Burren in the south, rock upland; it seems strange to find the same material building quite different shaped mountains here in the north. The reason seems to be that the underlying strata of the Ben Bulben group is soft and was undercut by weathering and especially by the grinding pressure of the ice which once filled the hollows between the mountains. That undercutting meant rock falls and the making of precipice features—landslips following the ice melt produced the beautiful little "Swiss Valley" in Glen Car, near which a stream descends the rocks in a series of cascades with the delightful name of *Sruth in aghaidh an Aird*, the stream against the height.

The flora of the Ben Bulben cliffs may well be a pre-glacial relict one. The summits themselves are flat and grassy with some heather on little patches of peat, which also seems to be a relic, this time of a once more general cover of peat. It is worth listing some of the plants of these limestone hills of Sligo and Leitrim to indicate something of the beauty and interest to be found upon the ledges of the grey rock. The Ben Bulben group, then, is the only British station of the Fringed Sandwort, *Arenaria ciliata*. It is the only Irish station of the alpine saxifrage, *Saxifraga nivalis*, and the chickweed wintergreen, *Epilobium alsinefolium*. These three plants are all arctic alpines.

The other plants to be found include: alpine meadow rue (*Thalictrum alpinum*), alpine scurvy grass (*Cochlearia alpina*), hoary whitlow grass (*Draba incana*), northern rockcress (*Arabis petraea*), moss campion (*Silene acaulis*), mountain avens (*Dryas octapetala*), purple saxifrage (*Saxifraga oppositifolia*), yellow saxifrage (*Saxifraga aizoides*), roseroot (*Sedum rosea*), viviparous polygonum (*Polygonum viviparum*), wood bedstraw (*Galium sylvestre*), alpine enchanter's nightshade (*Circaea alpina*), eyebright (*Euphrasia salisburgensis*), mountain sorrel (*Oxyria digyna*), blue sesleria (*Sesleria caerulea*), green spleenwort (*Asplenium viride*), holly fern (*Polystichum lonchitus*) and maidenhair fern (*Adiantum capillus-Veneris*). The woods on the lower slopes are a remnant of the old native Irish woodland cover of the country.

The tufts of alpines on the precipices of these limestone hills, rooted in the clefts of the rocks, reminds one of a story of the sacking of the Dominican priory in Sligo town, a story which is a good illustration of the sudden sheerness of these mountain cliffs.

The graceful ruins of the Dominican priory, founded in 1252, still stand in Sligo, not very far from the modern Dominican church. As in many parts of Ireland, the Reformation legislation failed in its attempt to end the religious life and here in Sligo the friars continued, off and on, to live in their house, and to minister to the people. It was dangerous but it was done.

But in the rising of 1641, Sir Frederick Hamilton burned both Sligo and the priory of the Holy Cross. The account tells how the Protestant soldiers came into Sligo from Manorhamilton, and their own report relates:

> The Friars themselves were also burned, and two of them running out were killed in their habits. Wearisome was our march, and hot our service in our burning that night of the town of Sligo, where it is confessed by themselves that we destroyed more than three hundred people by fire, sword or drowning, to God's everlasting honour and glory and our own comfort.

Their own comfort also required a guide back over the hills in the darkness. The soldiers had stripped the dead friars of their white habits and they put one of them on a man they forced to act as a guide to Manorhamilton so that they could see him easily in the dusk. He led them in amongst the limestone mountains. Then he quickened his pace and broke into a run. The soldiers fired, missed, urged their horses after him over the upland. In a moment, they crashed to their deaths over the rim of one of the limestone cliffs. The guide went over the sudden lip of the precipice too, but he knew the ground and saved himself by leaping down to catch hold of a tree growing out from a crevice in the rock.

Ben Bulben, too, is one of those places where the death of Diarmaid in a boar hunt has been localised, and, returning to authentic history, its seaward slopes are the site of a foundation of St. Columcille at Drumcliff, where still stands the stump of a round tower and a noble Celtic High Cross. Near by, in 561, was fought the Battle of the Books, at Cuildrevne, in which St. Columcille's kinsmen successfully routed the forces of the High King of Ireland, after the High King had given judgment against Columcille and for St. Finbar of Moville, whose new revised text of Scripture Columcille had copied without permission. Part of the disputed work, the psalter called the *Cathach* ("Battle Book"), still exists and used to be carried as a talisman bringing victory by the O'Donnells. The evidence suggests that it is very probable that this ancient MS. is the one written by Columcille.

Immediately out to sea is the small flat island of Inishmurray, a green plat of limestone, and to sail out to it is to see one of the finest Celtic church sites still standing in Ireland: a group of old churches and beehive cells and a great collection of cross slabs, a monastery set within a massive stone *rath* donated by the local chief to St. Muredach when he sought a place for an island foundation. But the island is also one of the finest view-points from which to look at the mountains circling Donegal Bay, to Nephin and Mayo in the south, to the limestone heights immediately to the east and to Donegal in the north, a great semicircle of hills set between blue water, white-flecked, and blue sky, cloud-dappled.

And so the road goes on beyond Ben Bulben and north to Donegal town, with the slight ruins of the friary of the Four Masters set beside a peaceful inlet of the sea. From thence, the way is open into the Donegal highlands. Eastward, perhaps, over the upland to Lough Derg of St. Patrick's Purgatory, with the spread of the mountains at one's back and the promise of the island-dotted Lough Erne ahead; or north, through the broad windgap of Barnesmore for Letterkenny and Derry; or westward, to Malin More by the coast road, climbing and twisting and snaking up and down between rock and sea and hill, cliff and small strand. The Donegal hills form a great inland mass of heathery upland rising here and there into striking mountain forms, of which the white peak of Errigal in the north and the great cliff of Slieve League in the south are the most impressive. The rocks are the Dalradian schists, continuing across from Scotland, with granite of Caledonian Age in the Rosses and Tory Island, and of Tertiary age in the Barnesmore Gap. The whole country is deeply printed with the NE.–SW. grain produced by the Caledonian mountain-building movements: it stands out almost diagrammatically from the survey maps in the long lines of the glens and the intervening hill ridges.

The mountains themselves form a kind of crescent whose horns face the sea, and based upon the Blue Stack group north of Donegal town. One horn is formed by Slieve Tooey and Slieve League, the other in the north by Errigal and the Derryveagh mountains. Cupped between them, facing the sea, is the low country about Ardara and Gweebarra Bay and the Rosses, where the land is all littered with great rocks, some of which are as big as the cottages beside them. It is a beautiful oasis, this lowland in the circle of the Donegal mountains, where the pale gold of the primroses covers all the dunes at the back of the sandy beaches in springtime. It is, nearly all of it, lowland and hill alike, rough, "mountainy" country, with small farms and the people thickly congregated on the little arable land that is to be had. It is a country of great sea cliffs, battered by wild winter storms, with the salt spray driving far inland, so that one may come on unexpected patches of salt-loving plants where other things would be scorched by the sea winds. Sea cliffs are an essential part of the scene and Tory Island, nine miles out in the Atlantic, has some of the finest cliff scenery in the whole of Ireland.

Impressions are perhaps always too general; but of Donegal I would say that it has about it a clean clearcutness as distinct from the other Irish mountain districts. There is a bright sheen in its light, a sharpness in its people's voices, a trimness in its cottages. These last are snuggled on the hillsides, longer and whiter than the southern homesteads, with the thatch bound down against the wind with ropes. Often there is a weaving shed included in the length of the house—house, plus shed, plus byre; for Donegal tweeds are famous and their weaving an important part of the economy of the district.

Thatched white cottages—a Scandinavian scholar has said that the Irish thatch is the finest peasant roof in Europe—old customs, the Irish speech retained amongst the hills. . . . The bog "fir" was used till recently for most constructional purposes here—the tree roots and trunks found in the peat cuttings. The flail is still used sometimes to thresh corn. Professor Estyn Evans, who has made so close a study of Irish homesteads and customs, has described the villages under Errigal as "archæological fossils". So they are, if you judge by externals as the archæologist and antiquarian must, but the people themselves are living in today. The radio set is placed near the archaic-looking open fireplace. If the material background is still poor, it has resulted in making the men who live there more resourceful and more enterprising than those who live in easier country. It is the mark of the "mountainy" man everywhere that you feel that he sees reality and sees it whole.

From Donegal town the road leads west by the important fishing harbour of Killybegs (*na Cealla beaga*, the little churches) and on through Kilcar (*Cill Chártha*, St. Carthach's Church) to Carrick (*An Charraig*, the rock). It is a fascinating road, between hill and sea, and at Carrick one may turn down beside the long inlet of the sea that winds inland and go to the hamlet of Teelin to make the ascent of Slieve League.

From Teelin there is a good track all the way up the mountain and the first mile or so is possible for a car. The track curves up along the flank of a valley which bites far into the mass of the mountain and from its head one comes out with little exertion upon the summit levels. This is the old pilgrim track, and, I was told, once the main route over to Malin More.

All Donegal is hedged about with ancient things; beyond Carrick the Celtic crosses and site of Glencolumbkille (the glen of St. Columcille's church) which still honours its patron with a pilgrimage on June 9th; at Gartan, the birthplace of the same saint; at Teelin, another famous pilgrim station; so too at the Doon Well. And from prehistory, close to Malin More is a fine horned cairn called the Cloughanmore. The summit of Slieve League (*Sliabh leic*, the mountain of flagstones, 1972 feet) has a spring of water, now a holy well, and the ruins of a Celtic hermitage. The saints associated with it are St. Assicus, one of St. Patrick's companions who is said to have been a skilled metal worker, and later on, St. Hugh MacBric, a bishop who died in 588. There used to be a great pilgrimage up the mountain, but it is now only made by individuals occasionally and on their own.

But this pilgrim track is the easy way up Slieve League and the right route is by the rumpled line of cliffs above the sea, which narrow at the One Man's Pass to a ribbon of quartzite, about two feet wide, with a drop to the glen of the pilgrim track on the one hand, and to the sea on the other. There is another narrow section, as you continue on over the summit and down to Malin More, but it is broader and called therefore the Old Man's Path.

These cliffs, descending nearly 2000 feet to the sea, are perhaps the finest in mainland Ireland. There are other lesser cliffs on the north side of the mountain too, cradling the corrie lake of Lough Agh, and on them the botanists have reported the most varied collection of alpines to be found in the Donegal hills.

The summit is fascinating; the hermitage beside its well, snuggled in a hollow against the sea winds; and from the top itself, the outlook over all Donegal Bay. It is an outlook suggested to one as one drives the road from Donegal to Carrick, with glimpses across the sea to Mayo and the massive lump of Nephin and to the limestone hills of Ben Bulben. But from Slieve League the whole bay is spread beneath with its ringing mountains, and in clear weather one may, so it is claimed, see Croagh Patrick.

Most of the mountain is of the Donegal schists, but the summit has a small outcrop of Carboniferous rocks, indicating how the later strata must once have covered all these high hills, themselves to be later almost entirely stripped away by erosion. On Slieve League, too, is a trace of the highest of the Irish peneplain surfaces, at nearly 2000 feet above the sea. Other peneplain levels are indicated by the moors from which Errigal springs (at about 1000 feet) and the Rosses (200 feet).

The variety of rock building the mountain makes the cliffs a variegated pattern of differently coloured crags, with runs of heather and grass between. Perhaps the whole line of cliffs is best seen not from the mountain-top, but by scrambling over the moorland from Teelin out to Scregeighter Head, from which the whole line is laid before one right to Malin Beg and Rathlin O'Birne Island just off the coast. In this rough moorland, with its little rocky hills and small lakes, I found the pink butterwort (*Pinquicula lusitanica*). Rock pinnacles and some offshore stacks diversify delicious descents to the clear sea, and with a certain goat-like agility there are many possible adventurous scrambles and traverses to be made amongst these cliffs. The whole line was traversed by H. C. Hart at a level of 1000 feet above the sea,

17 The ridge and sea cliffs of Slieve League, Co. Donegal

18 Ben Bulben, Co. Sligo

19 The skyline of the Donegal hills including Errigal

SLIEVE TOOEY

a journey which took him three days. Hart was the first to explore the Donegal mountains for the purpose of making a botanical survey of them which he carried out in 1883-4. He gave an amusing description of part of his Slieve League climbing:

> There is a track to the sea at one place between the Eagle's Nest and the One Man's Pass. While scrambling along the sea face I came on this track amongst the steep heather, bracken and bear berry, and a bare footprint induced me to follow it to the water's edge. Considerably above the sea the track had disappeared, but I could still notice footholds on the almost vertical rock, and finally appeared an old man and a little boy emerging from the ocean brink. They were loaded with samphire, which they ate as they rested in their climb, and were vastly surprised at my appearance— the only stranger they had ever seen there, and they besought of me to go no farther with my boots on! I have never before found the peasants using raw samphire as food. Boiled with milk it is supposed to cure a cold. This track is called Thone-na-culliagh.

Mountain-climbing is still not so popular in Ireland that you will not meet with surprise. "Where," cried out an old man of his son, whom I had met as I came down the Twelve Bens on a rather wild and misty day, "did you raise the woman?"

Something of the same kind of cliff scenery is found upon Slieve Tooey (*tuaith*, north, 1458 feet) which rises to the north of Glencolumbkille. It is a mere heather walk up from the little farms on its slopes out on to its summit, but the mountain faces the sea in cliff and gully and offshore stack, where the water comes in black depths shading to jade greens which make the quartzite boulders seen through its shallows look green likewise. The peat upon the ridge itself is weathered into fantastic stacks (in spite of the rain of Ireland today, the peat (turf) is not now being formed but is in many places being eroded). There is a small blue lake hidden in the fold of Slieve Tooey and a great outlook up the coast to the north, to the sands of Gweebarra Bay and to the mountains beyond it. If you work on along the ridge and round to the south of the summit you come upon a beautiful lake encircled by cliffs and named Lough Anaffrin, the lake of the Mass. Here Mass was said in Penal times. There is another very different Mass site between the Donegal mountains and those of Ben Bulben—a cave in the rock by the river side, below the ruins of the Cistercian abbey of Assaroe.

Between Slieve Tooey and Slieve League is the green oasis of Glencolumbkille, with the mighty cliffs of Glen Head and the Sturrall Rock, and the sandy strand between the rocks, backed by dunes with little white Scots roses and stately yellow flags. It is a good country this, cliff and sea and the clean white sand; small white cottages set each on its holding on the flanks of the hills. It is a country Irish-speaking and rich in Irish traditions, together with other stories like the one that Prince Charles took refuge here and of the Spanish churches built with money from a ship wrecked on the cliff foot of Slieve League.

Northward, out of Glencolumbkille, the road descends Glengesh Hill, one of the steepest roads in Ireland, to Ardara and so on across the Rosses, to Errigal (19), the highest point in Donegal, 2466 feet. Perhaps it is the most striking of the Irish peaks, a sudden white pyramid of quartzite springing up solitary from the plain. Two smaller summits lie across Altan Lough (*Altán*, little cliff) from it, Aghla More and Aghla Beg (*eachla*, an enclosure for horses, a stable, which may have existed on the low ground. *Mor* is large and *beag* small). Then there is the deep cut of Muckish Gap and rounded like the back of a hog, the mass of Muckish Mountain (*Muc ais*, pig's back) (16) to the north of it, rising to 2197 feet. The name of Errigal itself was apparently originally *Airecal Adhamhnain*, the house or oratory of St. Adamnan, Columcille's biographer, and like the latter a Donegal man. Very likely there was a small church of his in this area, which is now lost sight of.

All these mountains rise in line, symmetrically from the moors (you may see them across the sea from Tory Island in a magnificent array of peaks), but though all of them satisfy the eye it is always Errigal in its white purity that attracts beyond the others. I saw it first in spring, in the haze of a May heatwave, when the dusty roads were all edged with the fire and flame of scented gorse that set off the whiteness of the mountain. Below, in the glen, one could get out of the glare in Dunlewy Church (*Dún Lughaidh*, Ludaidh's fort) and standing in its porch beside the modern round tower that serves for belfry, look up at the loveliness of Errigal immediately above.

From far off, even from Dunlewy Church, those long white

screes falling from the white ridge look dangerous and difficult, but there is a back door to Errigal—the road past Dunlewy climbs high on to the moors behind the mountain, and a walk over rising ground from this same road takes one first high on to the end of the ridge of Errigal, and then, with a brief scramble over scree and rock, on to the summit itself. That top is an aerial but safe enough undulating ridge, the screes falling away on either hand, with broken pinnacles of quartzite here and there. All the world is spread below, lakes sparkling both on the low ground and high on the mountains too, on the Derryveagh Ridge. The lake under Aghla More has yellow beaches, whilst on the other side, the lake in Dunlewy glen I saw shot with wind-driven ripples, whilst the glen's green woods contrasted with the brown of the moors and the yellow ribbons of the roads. Across from Errigal rises the long grey quartzite ridge of the Derryveagh mountains (*Doire bheathach,* birch wood) (1) with the Poisoned Glen leading into their heart, country much like the Twelve Bens, with bare rock summits looking from above like the wrinkled hide of some petrified elephant. The name Poisoned Glen is mysterious (the valley itself is the continuation of the Dunlewy hollow); it has been suggested that it was so called because the poisonous Irish spurge grew there. The Derryveagh mountains provide rock-climbing; their highest point is Slieve Snacht (*Sliabh snechta,* mountain of snows, 2240 feet). There is another Slieve Snacht, 2019 feet, in Donegal, in the mountain backbone of the isolated Inishowen peninsula, the long neck of land lying between the sea inlets of Loughs Foyle and Swilly, and terminating in Malin Head, again not to be confused with the Malin More headland in Glencolumbkille.

Errigal is bare of vegetation, except for scraps of club moss amongst the rocks. During the glacial period, it is thought the ice first covered the mountain entirely (which means an ice sheet at the least 2500 feet thick), but that later the peak stood up above the snows in rugged isolation. The Derryveaghs show intense ice smoothing in their rounded heights.

The little stony roads of Donegal take one exploring amongst all these mountains, through Muckish Gap, or in the opposite direction to Gartan, the birthplace of St. Columcille (Columba) in 521. The road leads from Muckish Gap to Gartan past the foot of the long and narrow Lough Beagh (the birch lake), cradled amongst high cliffs and with pines to frame it at its foot, water far more Scottish than Irish in appearance, and then still going toward the east, comes to Lough Gartan, an entire contrast, a placid open stretch of water set amongst woods and fields which are of an entirely different and quieter aspect than those of the mountain country a few miles away.

The main road from Letterkenny to Dunfanaghy (*Dún Fionna chon*, the fort of Finn chu) runs parallel to this small Muckish–Gartan road, but farther to the north-east. From it one may explore out to the cliffs of Horn Head, or out to Fanad Head (*Fanad*, sloping ground) which terminates the shore of Lough Swilly opposite the Inishowen peninsula. This Dunfanaghy–Letterkenny road passes through a fine rocky defile called the Barnesbeg Gap, which recalls in its name the much larger gap that carries the road north from Donegal town to Letterkenny through the great inland mass of the Donegal hills, the Barnesmore Gap. The name is from *Bearnas*, a gap. The Barnesmore Gap was an important strategic pass (and therefore battleground) leading into Donegal and the territory of the O'Donnells.

You can study much of the north of Donegal from two historic places, the Doon Rock, and Grianan of Ailech. The latter (15) is a round stone fort, the palace or *grianan* (with the original meaning of a sunny spot) of Ailech, set on the ridge above Derry, where Lough Swilly, the lake of the sallows, winds far inland amongst the hills and the fields. The Doon Rock is a knob of rock in the uplands between Gartan and Kilmacrenan; it commands a striking prospect of little fields which lead up to the more rugged little mountain-tops of north Donegal. Below the rock is the holy well of Doon. The rock was the inauguration place of the O'Donnells and here came Red Hugh after his escape from Dublin Castle to take up his formal leadership of his people.

From Red Hugh O'Donnell's return to Donegal in 1592 stems the exciting and tragic story of the last attempts of the Irish chiefs to hold Gaelic Ireland for the Irish by organised force of arms. Red Hugh led various expeditions into Connacht between 1595 and 1597 and he was present at the Irish victory at the Battle of the Yellow Ford in 1598. Then came the disaster of the muddle and defeat of the Irish and the expeditionary force of

Spaniards at Kinsale in 1601. That meant the end of the Irish hopes and the beginning of the great plantations of Ulster.

Red Hugh fled to Spain in 1602, where he died at Valladolid the same year. A Franciscan from Donegal attended his deathbed there, and Donegal indeed is closely associated with the Franciscan Order. In the ruin following Kinsale, it was Franciscan initiative that set about trying to collect all the surviving Irish MSS. to preserve Irish history and literature for posterity. It is the Donegal friary that is associated with the names of the Four Masters who carried out this work, Brother Michael O'Clery, the chief of the group, Cúcoigcríche O'Clery, Fearfeasa O'Mulconry and Cúcoigcríche O'Duignan. Michael O'Clery tirelessly travelled Ireland copying, always copying, every Irish manuscript that he could find, a tremendous work of scholarship and journeying. In the town of Donegal now stands the fine memorial church of the Four Masters, a good example of modern Irish Romanesque architecture executed in granite from the Barnesmore Gap. And the Franciscans are lately back in Donegal, with a new friary at Rosnowlagh.

In 1607 came the Flight of the Earls, the beginning of the long series of wild geese to leave their country. It seems very probable that these wild geese were right in their going—that had they stayed one by one they might have been blended into the matrix of the English ascendancy, but that in going they kept their Irishness and their faith and their determination, and not only theirs, but that of the folk at home who watched their exploits from far off. And the returned soldier of fortune was the obvious hard core of local resistance.

Donegal saw some of the action of the rising of 1798. It was into Lough Swilly that the French ship *Hoche* brought Wolfe Tone and a party of 300 Frenchmen to aid the Irish. The ship and the men aboard were both captured; Wolfe Tone died in prison before the sentence of execution could be carried out on him.

So then all this Donegal country is interwoven with history, from the legends of the giant Balor that the Tory islanders will still tell you, and the horned cairns, from Gartan of Columcille, from the Doon Rock and Red Hugh, to the Odyssey of the Four Masters, the Mass Rocks hidden in the hills and the stories of the priests who served them, Franciscans among them, living "on their keeping" in the mountain wilderness. And on the island in Lough Derg, St. Patrick's Purgatory, the last stronghold of the ancient penitential routine of the Church, is each year attracting bigger crowds to do penance and pray in the silence of the Donegal uplands.

Yet perhaps the essence of the country for the mountaineer is that clearness and purity of line and colour that is typical of Donegal, the sheer cliffs of Glen Head and the bright sands between them with the sea breaking on them; the white cone of Errigal rising from the roads edged with the gold of the gorse, the small white cottages set amongst their stone-walled fields under the line of the high ridges.

CHAPTER IV

The Burren

In springtime Ireland is gilded with the flowers of the gorse. The hillsides are aflame with it, the boreens heady with its scent. The whipped cream of the blackthorns, white flowers on dark leafless boughs, contrasts vividly with the rich gold. But in West Clare, in the Burren, there is a sudden change, the gorse bushes fail and the blackthorns rule undisputed, like garlands of sea spume twisted over the hills and lanes.

The Burren (*Boireann*, a stony, rocky district)(22) is the northern half of the great bulge of the western coast of Ireland between Galway Bay and Shannon Mouth. Here, a Cromwellian soldier is said to have noted a local proverb that there is no tree from which to hang a man and no water in which to drown him, furthermore, no soil in which to bury the body when the problem of killing him is solved. For Burren is a limestone "karst", where the Carboniferous limestone rises into hills, rounded and bare unlike those of Ben Bulben to the northward, but now and again with cliffs and sheer walled valleys. At the mouth of Galway Bay the Aran Islands continue the same pattern of bare grey limestone country, with sheer sea cliffs, the islands ending against the Atlantic in a sudden mighty drop, just as the mainland cliffs of Moher in Co. Clare fall in one drop of 668 feet. Between the rocks and in the valleys there is fertile soil and a brilliance of wild flowers unrivalled in the whole country. The streams make their way underground, there are sudden swallow holes, and in summer the hilltops are parched, so that the ordinary pattern of mountain pasturing is reversed, and the cattle go to the tops in winter, not in summer, when they would have nothing to drink. The winter climate is mild, frost almost unknown, and the limy land builds sturdy bones in the beasts that graze it.

The Burren is small, about 50 square miles, and its highest

hill is only the 1134 feet of Slieve Elva. Yet it is a country hard to forget, with its crisp clean colours, white and green like the Irish tricolour, with the orange of the gorse eliminated. White rock dazzling in the sun, stone walls criss-crossing the land, stone forts, ruined churches, the castle of Kinvarra set by the sea, and across Galway Bay the line of the Twelve Bens, the bright blue sea flecked with wave crests and the brown and blue of distant Connemara.

It is indeed from the farther side of Galway Bay that one may gain the best introduction to the Burren hills, looking across to them from the coast road out to Spiddal, and seeing the clean rock of their terraced hills rising in an undulating line from the massif of Black Head at the bay's mouth east to Kinvarra. With every change of light the limestone rock alters and reflects the weather's moods, now grey and dull, now pink, now picking up the blue of the sea in the haze of evening, or flashing silver with the wet of a passing shower. To approach closer, by Kinvarra and to Ballyvaghan, and the Lisdoonvarna road which clambers in a lariat of corkscrews over the hills, is to discover a land of rock, grey rock in slabby karst plateaux, with deep clefts weathered out along the joints between the slabs, grey rock in terraced features which show the bedding of the rock like some gigantic geological diagram, and beneath the cliffs, the grey rock in littered screes.

The valleys, like the amphitheatre of Ballyvaghan, are green and fertile, the orchards hung with rosy apples, and so are the strips of soil between the rocks. As in the Aran Islands, these small plots of rich soil carry many flowers, and they can survive there even in the thinnest skin of earth because the climate is wet enough to prevent it drying out completely. And in Burren the ordinary pattern of plant distribution is forgotten; the climber on the rocks finds not only the intermingled Lusitanian and American species but the alpines, all growing together and extending down to the sea cliffs from the heights.

Late spring sees the Burren flowers at their best. The blackthorn has faded to a shabby brown, but the hawthorns have taken over and every cliff is now decorated with the white, or often pale pink, May blossom, set off by its glossy leaves. On the short turf is the vivid blue of the tiny spring gentian (*Gentiana verna*) and the white of the mountain avens (*Dryas*

20 Cloudscape over the Mourne mountains

21 Sunset over Galway Bay and the hills of the Burren

22 Typical Burren country—Mullagh More, Co. Clare

23 The early Christian stone 'fort' of Cahercommaun in the Burren

octapetala) which flowers off and on all summer, ending in the autumn with its silky ornamental seeds. Tufts of saxifrage cling to the rocks and to the walls of the old forts. There is the Mediterranean orchid (*Neotinea intacta*, dense spiked orchid) and the maidenhair fern (*Adiantum capillus Veneris*) which is found as far south as the tropics, and it is growing in the crevices of rocks with arctic alpines! Here are brilliant displays of cranesbill (*Geranium sanguineum*, the bloody cranesbill); tufts of wild thyme, the gold of eggs-and-bacon, the pink and blue milkworts, the yellow hawkweeds, and many more.

It is not all bare rock and short flower-speckled turf. There is a suggestion of once much more extensive woods in the relict woodland types found in the clefts between the rocks, the strangely dwarfed scrub of blackthorn here and there apart from its more normal growth over most of the area, and then the honeysuckle and ivy mingling with the green straps of the hart's tongue ferns in the joints of the limestone. Then there are the thick woods of hazel in the valleys and below the cliffs, there are yews and junipers, and there are tall spindle trees which in autumn turn vivid crimson red, their leaves like torches blazing against the duller greens and yellows of the coppice and their seeds pink with orange teeth. The little white Scots rose (*Rosa spinosissima*) is everywhere, another relict of woodland long destroyed, in autumn adding to the colour of the scene with its red hips. And here too are luxuriant juicy blackberries for the picking in autumn.

It is probable that once, as in the Aran Islands, the woods were more extensive and the bare rock covered. There seems also to have been some more extensive cover of peat and heather, for there are still little relict plots of peat with a growth of ling upon them. And Slieve Elva, the highest point, is a long ridge of a hill whose level top is a wet moss with extensive peat cuttings in it.

These Burren plants have in fact been described as "the most remakable assemblage of diverse types to be found in Ireland",[*] and it may therefore be worth listing some of the other species to be found. Northern or highland types, found growing down to sea-level, include vernal sandwort (*Arenaria verna*), stone bramble (*Rubus saxatilis*), cut-leaved saxifrage (*Saxifraga hypnoides*) and bearberry (*Arctostaphylos uva-ursi*).

[*] R. Lloyd Praeger, *Natural History of Ireland*, 1950.

There is also the shrubby potentilla (*Potentilla fruticosa*), northern bedstraw (*Galium boreale*), bugle (*Ajuga pyramidalis*), wild madder (*Rubia peregrina*), rockrose (*Helianthemum canum*), helleborine (*Epipactis atropurpura*) and broomrape (*Orobanche rubra*).

I climbed Slieve Elva in September, a time when the moor rushes are cut to thatch turf rick and stack. Rushes of this sort grow on the heights of Slieve Elva, and a little troop of donkeys were engaged in bringing them down, piled high in panniers. Donkeys on a job can be left to pick their own way, and their pannier baskets emptied at the farm below, they were tripping slowly back along the road and then up the hillside track on their own, whilst their owner came after them at his leisure in the rear. This particular day was one of great clearness, so that from the marshy wetness of the top of Slieve Elva I looked not only across to the bare rocks and terraced features of the Black Head—Cappanawalla hills fronting Galway Bay—but far beyond, so that it almost seemed that this low ridge of Elva looked to all the hills of Ireland. For across Galway Bay lay the heights of Connemara and in contrast, rising from the flat bog by the coast, the low stumps of Roundstone and Doon hills. Inland one could see Nephin, and looking south, over to Slieve Aughty and the Galtees and across Shannon Mouth to Mount Brandon and the Dingle peninsula. Out to sea lay the Aran Islands, with their white sandy beaches gleaming in the sunshine and the little houses on Inisheer clear and distinct.

It is small and compact, this Burren, and from Elva I could drive across to the foot of Cappanawalla (1024 feet) and go up through coppice and pasture out on to its flat summit slabs on which bootnails slipped and skidded. One saw red hawthorn berries against the pale rock, the blue bloom of sloes, and nuts to be picked from the hazels; the boggy patches with the white flowers of grass of parnassus, the bronze seed spikes of bog asphodel, the drier plots with ling heather in flower, and great sheets of the violet-blue devil's bit scabious; in autumn the Burren was still bright with flower and seed. From Cappanawalla one looks directly down on the sea, the tide was far out in the bay of Ballyvaghan, mud flat and strand and islet, and the tempered colours of the gathering depths.

I passed a round stone fort going up this hill, and all the

Burren is littered with these remains, built in the nearest and most abundant material to hand, stone. Stone forts in this area in fact number thousands and indicate how in Celtic times the place was well populated and engaged in raising cattle on the hills. Strictly they are not "forts", but defendable farmsteads, whose stone walls, sometimes concentric, made a safe lodging for man and beast against marauders and wolves. Not all the forts would have been occupied at the same time. One of them, dating from c. A.D. 800, has been fully excavated. It is Cahercommaun (*caher*, a stone fort), a semicircular fort set on the side of one of the steep Burren cliffs, about $4\frac{1}{2}$ miles north of Corofin. You approach from Carran, by one of the little dusty Burren roads, in summer travelling in a column of swirling grey limestone dust that penetrates the most dustproof car, in winter splashing through grey sticky mud. The cliff feature rises in front, with another stone fort set on its brow. Cahercommaun lies to the east of this and may be gained by walking along the edge of the cliff from the roadside.

Like the great stone fort of Dun Aengus in the Aran Islands, this Clare fort is a semicircle, with the cliff forming one of its defensive lines. Within a solidly built wall were found a group of small stone huts in which its inmates lived; outside are two concentric walls of slighter masonry in which the cattle could be herded at night. From the chief's hut inside there is an underground passage, a souterrain, which provided an emergency escape to the cliff face. The finds showed something of the life in Co. Clare in early ninth-century times, the people were cattle-raising farmers—the excavators found some 9000 lb. of animal bones and the majority were those of the ox. Saddle and rotary querns indicated grain growing, and the absence of pottery the use of wooden vessels—a long-standing Irish custom, to be linked with the presence of woodland. So today, inside the hillside cottage in treeless places like Donegal and Mourne, you see churn and tub of staves of wood, perhaps of staves of the bog fir bound with willow bands. The Clare people smelted the iron for their implements and weapons on the spot: these settlements were largely self-supporting in such things. The place could hold out against a brief attack, but not for very long as it had no water supply, the present-day nearest wells being half a mile off.

The bones and the charcoal from the fires tell us something more—of the presence of the horse and the sheep and the pig in small numbers, of deer hunted on the hillsides (and at the old Celtic site of Oughtmama, these Burren deer are shown fighting with antlers interlocked on the holy water stoop within the door of the principal church). Bird bones included the now extinct white-tailed eagle. The people also went down to the sea and brought back supplies of shellfish to eat. On their fires they burned the wood from the surrounding forest, hazel and yew, ash and hawthorn, prunus, willow and elm.

Since the rock is the same, these Clare forts are very like the more famous ones of Aran. At Ballykinvarga is another large fort with a *chevaux de frise*, or "tank trap" of modern days, of limestone fragments set on edge outside the wall, just as they are placed outside Dun Aengus and Dubh Cathair in Aran. They are still hard to walk through quickly. The occupation of the area has been continuous from prehistoric times. The ruins of Megalithic cairns stand on the hillsides, then come the stone forts, one of which near Ballykinvarga, Cahermacnaghten was inhabited by the family of O'Davoren and their law school down to the end of the seventeenth century. Structurally primitive, their culture rose to great artistic heights, as witness the silver brooch and other ornaments found at Cahercommaun and the splendid gold gorget found at Gleninsheen near Ballyvaghan, hidden in a crevice of the rock.

It was Burren of the saints too, with the Celtic foundation of St. Enda just out across the bay in Aran, and here in Clare are many old church sites. There is a fine Romanesque doorway at Dysert O'Dea and a high cross, and there is another high cross at the old church of Kilfenora; then down in the flat below the limestone hills, on the road towards Gort, there is the cluster of old churches of Kilmacduagh (MacDuach's Church), with the round tower leaning well out of the perpendicular. Kilmacduagh is the foundation of the great Clare saint, Colman MacDuach, whose dates are around the end of the sixth and beginning of the seventh centuries. Colman was in Aran first, and then in a hermitage under the Eagle's Cliff, Ceanaille, in Burren, before he founded Kilmacduagh and Oughtmama. Ceanaille is a great crag, rising from a ruff of thicket, amongst which the saint's well and the gable end of an old chapel are still to be found by careful searching amongst the undergrowth. Oughtmama is a rock-circled valley, green and fertile, high on the hills above Burren village, overlooking Galway Bay. Aengus the Culdee in his litany (A.D. 780) invokes the Seven Holy Bishops of Oughtmama in Corcomruadh. It long remained a place of pilgrimage, but the centre of ecclesiastical activity shifted downhill to the Cistercian foundation a short distance off. The shell of the great church still stands, as do the Oughtmama ones above. The Cistercian foundation was made in 1195, and lies in a fertile cup of land, set amongst a network of stone walls and hawthorn hedges, all white scented flowers in early summer—white rock, white flowers, white church. The Cistercians gave the church the lovely name of Sancta Maria de Petra Fertili, St. Mary's of the Fertile Rock.

Is this perhaps the very keynote of the Burren hills as the climber explores them, the rock that is indeed both bare and fertile? Flowers and stones, a grass most vividly green, the thickets of hazels floored with twayblade, hazels whose branches you must part to penetrate, of sparkling springs bearing perhaps the name of a Celtic saint, and always the tracks of men in cairn and caher and church and the maze of stone-walled fields. It is a country both desolate upon the first aquaintance and fertile upon the closer inspection, the rocky desert that not only blossoms as the rose but with the rose, the white Scots briars set in the clefts of the white rocks, white rocks that catch the colours of the sea and the sky and the sunset with every change of light.

CHAPTER V

The Height of Erin

IN a country like Ireland, of broad undulating plains, the smallest hill may take upon itself an importance that it could never have in more mountainous terrain. So it is that the Irish lowland has many small hills which both command vast outlooks across the fields and bogs, and whose names are linked with the great events of Irish history. Then, too, there are the lesser mountain ranges of the country, the Sperrin mountains in the north, the hills about Lough Derg on the lower Shannon, and the Slieve Blooms: the Height of Erin, as their highest point is named (26); they are in a way outside an account of the main Irish mountain groups and yet it seems impossible to write of Irish hills without some mention of these lesser heights.

It is the small hill in the plain or the large hill standing alone that is the most likely to have gathered around it tradition and legend. So the Finn cycle is attached to the isolated mountains of Slieve Gullion (25) in the north and Slievenamon in the south and to small rises like the Hill of Allen in the great flat bogs in Co. Kildare. Then, too, the lesser rise, above the marshy hollow, is the natural site for fort or church. Tara of the High Kings is on a slight rise, and so too many other old *raths* and churches, alone or together as they are found at Downpatrick. The well-drained slopes of these small hills, quite apart from defensive ideas, would attract settlement. There are, too, the inauguration places of the chiefs, often on hill or rock, like that of Doon in Donegal. It was on a hill, according to his own account, that St. Patrick began to love God and began his life of prayer; traditionally this hill is the 1437 feet of Slemish (*Sliabh Mis, mis* being a woman's name) (30) in Co. Antrim on which the young Patrick herded his master's beasts. And, later, it was on Saul (*Sabhal*, a barn) Hill that Patrick, returning to preach to the Irish, established his first church, on a low mound of a hill above

76

the mouth of Strangford Lough with an outlook across to the Mourne mountains to the south. From Saul he went south to Slane near Tara, on which he lit the Easter Fire at the beginning of his great mission. And Slane is a hill worth climbing, its 500 feet overlooking all the level richness of the pastures of Meath, its green fertility in utter contrast with the rock and moor of the western mountains.

In that same area of Slane and Tara and the great Megalithic tombs of the Boyne Valley, there are, farther to the west, beyond Kells, the low rise of the Slieve na Calliagh mountains, their highest point being only 911 feet above sea-level. On these uplands are thirty prehistoric burial cairns, a fine example of the way in which these structures were often placed both on great heights and on the highest ground to be found above the plains. Slieve na Calliagh (*Sliabh na Cailleghe*, the hag's mountain) stands alone and commands the central plain of Ireland. Many of the stones built into the cairns of the Bronze Age cemetery on it are decorated with geometrical designs like the cairns east of it in the Boyne Valley. There is another association with the area: Loughcrew, below the hills, was the birthplace of Blessed Oliver Plunket in 1629, later to be Archbishop of Armagh and to suffer martyrdom at Tyburn in 1681.

These cairns on the heights link with the old story about St. Patrick throwing down the stone circle of Crom Cruach at Mag Slécht in the Slieve Anieran (iron mountain) district, a structure described as the chief idol of Erin. Unfortunately for the story this particular stone circle seems to have been a recumbent one from its very building and the Patrician incident an invention to explain the way in which the twelve low boulders were arranged around a taller one which tilted over to the west. There never was a national idol of Crom Cruach or Croich.

What there was, was a long established cult of mountains: burials on the higher slopes and hilltops, and religious gatherings at these monuments. Later, the Celtic saints took over this instinct to look up to the hills, to climb for prayer and penance toward heaven, and built oratories upon the summits: Slieve League, Slieve Donard (where a Megalithic cairn was adapted to the new purpose), Croagh Patrick, Mount Brandon, and the hilltop pilgrimages became Christian ones to Christian shrines. But others seem to have been gatherings with no other end in view than a day's outing on the hills. Bilberry Sunday was an affair of picking bilberries (blaeberries), weaving baskets of rushes for the fruit and cages in which to enclose grasshoppers and butterflies that it was amusing to catch, a picnic in the fine summer weather. This day out, the first Sunday in August, has been kept up in some places up to modern times. It is interesting to note that the cages for the butterflies are part of a widespread custom that is mentioned by, for instance, the ancient Greek writers.

Of the less important groups of the Irish mountains, one might begin in the north, with the Sperrin mountains (*Cnoc speirín*, the pointed hills), a great inland upland area of Dalradian rocks, lying between Lough Foyle and the inland lake of Lough Neagh (29). They rise to 2240 feet in Sawel (*Sabhal*, a barn) Mountain, over whose crest runs the county boundary between Derry and Tyrone. One can leave the shores of Lough Neagh and drive cross-country through these hills, heading up from Cookstown in the hill-pass under Slieve Gallion (1735 feet) and coming of a sudden on Lough Fee, a little mountain lake with pines and rhododendrons and willows round about it. From there one looks across the main mass of the Sperrins, the road running over the moors and down into the valley of the Six Towns. The Sperrins are partly heathery, partly grassy; a great spread of boggy uplands.

From them one can go north to the coast and the famous coast road which runs from the Giant's Causeway round to Larne, and a different sort of hill scenery. This is the country of the Glens of Antrim (24), steep-sided valleys cut through the uplands formed by the lava flows of Tertiary volcanic activity: the coast road cliffs an extraordinary pattern of the brown or almost black basalt lava overlying the white chalk beneath it. The chalk was, by this overcoat of harder rock, preserved from erosion, and this part of Ireland is therefore important as the sole source of native flint (contained in the chalk) which the early settlers in the country could work up into artifacts. The uplands of this area rise to 1817 feet in Trostan, south-west of Cushendun, but the interest of the region is centred upon the cliffs and the road twisting along their foot, tunnelling now and again through the rock, and the deep glens which lead up from the coast. These are the famous Glens of Antrim and their

24 Glenariff, one of the 'Glens of Antrim'

25 Slieve Gullion and its forest park, Co. Armagh

26 The Slieve Bloom mountains

names read like a kind of Gaelic litany: Glentaise (*Taise Taobheal*, daughter of the king of Rathlin Island), Glenshesk (of the sedges), Glendun (of the fort), Glencorb (of the slaughtered), Glenaan (the little glen), Glenballyemon (of Edward's town), Glenariff (of the arable land), Glencloy (of the sword) and Glenarm (of the weapon).

Turning to the south, the Iron mountains may be mentioned again, for their name, Slieve Anieran, derives from the presence of clay ironstone in the rocks (Carboniferous) of which they are built. The area has been worked for iron at various times, and around Lough Allen shore there are many old furnace sites—one way in which the Irish woodland came to be destroyed. Not very far away, on the road from Sligo to Boyle and Carrick-on-Shannon, is the low ridge of the Curlew mountains, rising to only 860 feet but so placed on the road to Sligo that they have been of great importance in Irish history and the scene of a number of fights. The most famous of these Curlew Mountain battles was that of August 15th, 1599, when Red Hugh O'Donnell and Brian O'Rourke defeated the English forces under Sir Conyers Clifford. Earlier, in 1497, in a fight with the MacDermotts, the O'Donnells were defeated and lost their famous *Cathach*, which however they were able to recover two years later in another attack on MacDermott.

Over in the east, on the other side of Ireland, some small but striking hillocks rise from the plains around the Curragh and from the Bog of Allen, the 676 feet of the Hill of Allen, and the 768 feet of Dunmurry Hill and the Chair of Kildare. In early summer, or late spring, these little hills are bright with bluebells, primroses and violets on their flanks, Dunmurry in particular I remember for the show of yellow pansies in the short turf of its summit. The Hill of Allen is being deeply quarried for road metal.

Both these hills command enormous outlooks: over to the power station in the neighbouring bog producing electricity from the turf to the grassy plain of the Curragh rising out of the more boggy lower flats around it, to the round tower of Kildare of St. Brigit, and of course to the line of the Wicklow mountains to the east.

The Hill of Allen is one of the sites of the Finn stories. It is possible to distinguish three great localisations of the Finn cycle in Ireland, according to Prof. T. F. O'Rahilly: one in Munster, one in the Midlands, and one in this Allen area, a Laginian or Leinster Finn. This last had his principal *dun* on the Hill of Allen, which he had obtained from his grandfather— O'Rahilly regarded this as a watered-down version of the old saga theme of how the hero despoils the god of the underworld, here localised in the fairy hill or *sid* of Allen. There are a great many stories about these *sid* hills, into which mortals may sometimes penetrate to find the people of the fairy hill, engaged in an endless round of feast and festivity. So then *sid* or *sithean* is a frequent element in place-names here and in Scotland too, where the enormous bulk of Ben Tee (the mountain of the fairy hill) rises to 2957 feet above the central part of the Great Glen, showing the typical *sithean* shape to perfection.

Around Lough Derg, the southernmost of the Shannon lakes and not to be confused with Lough Derg of St. Patrick's Purgatory in Donegal, there is a large area of mountainous upland, west of the lake the Slieve Aughty mountains (*Sliabh Echtghe*, Echtghe —one of the mythological De Danna personages; highest point Cashlaundrumlahan, 1207 feet) and Slieve Bernagh mountains (*Sliabh bernach*, the gapped mountain; highest point Glennagalliagh, 1746 feet), east of it the Arra mountains (1517 feet). Farther east, the Golden Vale of Tipperary has for its northern boundary the hill country of the Slieve Felim and Silvermines mountains (rising to 2279 feet in Keeper Hill, Slievekemalta). North-east the hills extend into the ridge of the Devil's Bit mountains, and finally, an isolated group in the central plain between Birr and Portlaoighise (Maryborough) there are the Slieve Bloom mountains (*Sliabh Bladhma*, the mountain of Bladh; highest point Arderin, 1734 feet)(26). These uplands are all carved out of the upfolded Old Red Sandstone and underlying Silurian strata, the latter appearing in the cores of the folds whilst the hard sandstones form some of the prominent summits like the Devil's Bit and Keeper Hill. Southward, the line of the Irish mountains is controlled by the east–west trends of the Armorican folding, but north of the Golden Vale, the Caledonian NE.–SW. trends began to take control of the axes of folding and these hills show the same alignment as those to the north.

SLIEVE AUGHTY AND SILVERMINES

Perhaps the most striking impression of these uplands, through which the Shannon has to carve its way from the levels of the Central Plain to the open sea below Limerick, is gained by sailing up from that town to Lough Derg, when the river, and its canalised section above the powerhouse at Ardnacrusha, seem to be leading one into the depths of the hills—hills which are framed by the white concrete bridges spanning the canal section, symmetrical, like a Japanese painting. Entering Lough Derg is anticlimax, the hills fall away behind one, and the Shannon waterway meanders north over the inland plain, with the Slieve Blooms rising steeply from it, away to the east.

The Slieve Bernagh–Slieve Aughty country is rolling heather upland rather than mountain with small farms upon its slopes and little tracks of roads leading to them. There are pleasant lakes in the valleys, and some forestry plantations on their slopes leading up to the moors above. It is, in fact, an area somewhat isolated and off the main roads of Ireland and it seems that it was only comparatively lately settled. Prehistoric remains are largely absent, *Derry* place-names are frequent, and there seems to have been an immense oak wood covering the Slieve Aughty area down to Tudor times. This wood must have inhibited settlement. One cause of its eventual felling is to be found in the slag heaps of old iron furnaces that are to be found along the shore of Lough Derg and at Killaloe. There were tanneries here also, which would mean further destruction of the oak woods.

On the east side of Shannon the mountains are associated with Patrick Sarsfield's dramatic capture and destruction of the Williamite siege train at Ballyneety. That was in 1690, and it was on Keeper Hill that Sarsfield camped before his successful assault on the arms train. Again, it was over these mountains that O'Neill and O'Donnell marched on their way south to Kinsale and defeat in 1601. And the northern end of the district, the Silvermines mountains, is still a centre of lead and zinc mining. Silver occurs with the lead, and gave the name to the hills. The ore may have been known of and worked very early, mining operations are certainly known to have been in operation at the end of the thirteenth century. Fresh operations began again there in the seventeenth century, and both English and

Dutch miners worked there—some of them were killed in a fight in the 1641 rising. Boates' *Natural History by Several Hands* gives an account of the Silvermines of this period.

The veins of the mine commonly lay within three or four spits of the surface. They digged deeper as the veins went fathoms deep and then castle deep—the pits were not steep but sloping so it was possible to go in with barrows walking. The water seldom offended them as they were able to drain it into the river near by by conduits. The mine gave two different sorts of oar of which the most in quantity was of reddish colour, hard and glittering, and the other like a marl something blewish, and more soft than the red, and this was counted the best, producing most silver, whereas the other or glistening sort was very barren and went most away in litteridge or dross. The oar yielded one with another three pounds weight of silver out of each ton, but a great quantity of lead, so as that was counted the best profit to the farmer. Besides the lead and silver, the mine produced also some quicksilver but not any alom, vitriol, or antimony that I could hear of. The silver was very fine and sold in Dublin for 5s. 2d. the ounce sterling. The lead sold at the place for £11 sterling the ton or £12 at the City of Limerick. The King had the sixth part of the silver for his share and the tenth part of the lead, the rest remaining with the farmers whose profit was £2000 sterling yearly. All the mills, refining houses, melting houses, and other workhouses, stood within a quarter of a mile from the place where the mine is digged, every one of them conveniently built by the farmers or their substitutes.

Later operations at the mines seem to have been considerably less profitable than this old account might lead one to expect!

There is a small road which takes one through the heart of these mountains, Keeper Hill and the Silvermines to the north and Slieve Felim to the south, as it makes its way from Thurles to Newport overlooking the Shannon. It is rather open upland country, with the fields extending far up the hillsides, and the roadside banks all starred with primroses and violets in springtime—in Tipperary the violets grow thick enough to give a blue smirr to the hedgerow—and the skylarks singing constantly overhead.

It is not so much as mountains to climb that these hills are interesting, but as heights from which to survey the plains below or as the termination to the outlook across the level flats giving interest to a prospect otherwise dull. To travel the long

27 Fossil ripple prints in Old Red Sandstone rocks on the ridge of the MacGillycuddy Reeks, Co. Kerry

28 Pattern of hill farms on the slopes of the Paps of Dana, Co. Kerry

29 The Sperrin mountains

30 Slemish, the hill of St. Patrick's captivity, Co. Antrim

straight road from Cashel north to Portlaoighise is, in wet or misty weather, extraordinarily boring, but, when the skies are clear, the sudden rise and the brindled slopes of the Devil's Bit Mountain and the Slieve Blooms bring a fresh and continued interest.

The Devil's Bit, rising to 1577 feet, is a flat tableland leading to a sudden bit and then a small hummock of a rise continuing the summit line beyond it. Its proper name is *Bearnán Éile*, Eile's Gap. The *bearnán* does so much resemble a mouthful bitten out of a piece of bread that one may forgive the story of the devil snapping it out of Ireland and then spewing forth the untasty hunk again to form the Rock of Cashel in the plain of Tipperary! The story does not fit the rocks, for Cashel is a limestone bluff, and Devil's Bit summit, sandstone. Devil or no devil, Bearnán Éile is now under Our Lady's protection, for a great cross was set up on it to mark the Marian Year of 1954.

The Slieve Blooms, rising alone in the Central Plain, have a quite surprising importance for hills not 2000 feet high. They are seen from all the roads across the levels for long miles around, and it is not really so silly to have named their highest point Ard Erin, the height of Ireland. They were, in fact, long thought to be the real height and summit of Ireland, anyway by the people of the plains round them. They are a small group of rounded uplands, trending NE.-SW. for a dozen or so miles, and crossed by a high-level track from Kinnitty to Mountrath. West of them at Clareen is an old church site and a hawthorn, standing in the middle of the road, associated with St. Ciaran of Saigir, "first-born of the saints of Ireland", one of the pre-Patrician Irish saints and about whom many delightful stories are told of his friendship with the wild creatures of the woodlands on the slopes of these Slieve Bloom mountains.

The Slieve Blooms are important, too, as the source of three of the great Irish rivers. On them rises the Barrow, the Suir and the Nore, each taking different and lengthy circuits through Ireland, though all three eventually reach the sea at Waterford.

It comes as a shock, to those who suppose Ireland wet and mild in its climate, to record that I attempted to drive over the Slieve Blooms by the Kinnitty–Mountrath track in May and ended by sticking in a snow drift! It was unusual to have so much snow so late, but it came at the end of April and the beginning of May and then lay for a little in wet glistening wreaths upon all the southern mountains. The lowland, from which the hills rise suddenly, was green with the fresh spring leafage, the pastures were sprinkled with cowslips, and the woods with primroses and bluebells. Above them the heathery mountain-sides were patterned with streaks of snow.

There are extensive forestry plantations on the flanks of the hills, and the little track serves them. It climbs up from Kinnitty along the flank of the beautiful little valley of the Camcor River, pines mingling with leafing beeches and the like. Above, it is dark pine plantation and then the open moor over which the road runs straight and rather steeply, and across which lay, this particular May day, the broad backs of the drifts of snow, their melted water trickling down the track in a small stream. Looking back, the whole of the Central Plain and the flat course of the Shannon lies spread out, a vast inland sea of blue distances, as it seems. And that is perhaps the very essence of these lesser hills, this sense of being upon the height of Ireland, on an airy perch looking down upon the endless spread of bog and field and wood across which the rivers cut their wandering roads. The clouds move in majestic piles across the wide skies of these plains, and, far distant, is the rise of others of the Irish hills. It is a world spacious and sunlit, entirely different from the confining crags and narrow glens of higher mountains.

CHAPTER VI

The Leinster Chain

THERE is a dramatic moment on the road northward to Dublin from the south, when it comes out of Kildare on to the short turf of the Curragh, a grassy plain with sheep grazing amongst the gold flowered gorse bushes, and beyond it, lifting in a great line of heights, is the blue line of the Wicklow mountains.

Two of the great Irish mountain groups are built of granite, the Mournes of Tertiary and the Leinster chain of Caledonian Age. You may divide the Leinster chain into the Dublin hills in Co. Dublin, the main bulk, their continuation, the Wicklow hills (rising to 3039 feet in Lugnaquillia)(31) and in the south the Blackstairs and Mount Leinster (2610 feet), but essentially it is a single unit, a great structural feature in the bedrock of Ireland, a great arching fold in Ordovician and Silurian sediments into which granite was intruded, and which can be traced for 90 miles from Balbriggan north of Dublin down to the coast of Waterford. The actual outcrop of high ground is about seventy miles long, and the area some 625 square miles—the biggest outcrop of granite in Ireland and Britain.

They are hills quite different from the younger granite ones of Mournes, their summits rounded and mature in shape, a great undulating heather moor with hags and bogs and whilst it is the crest of the Mournes that attract, in the Leinster chain it is the valleys that are the great centre of interest and beauty.

The fold into which the granite was intruded is asymmetrical and the hills are so still, the west side cut by short and open valleys, the eastern by long trenches of glens. As a hill feature, they are old: the Leinster mountains provided pebbles for the Carboniferous sediments laid down below their heights. The Glacial period, too, has been studied closely in this area, and it seems that there were two general glaciations by large ice sheets—one such pushed across from Britain and deposited sea-shells from the channel floor on the Three Rock Mountain above Dublin: and in addition two, or perhaps three, mountain glaciations. When the granite was intruded into the sedimentary rocks its heat altered and hardened them to schists, and these metamorphic, altered sediments resisted erosion better than the granite which brought the change about. So it seems that the core of the range, where the granite was exposed, was more easily worn down than the glens below, which were wild ravines, narrowing as their streams descended from the hills to the plains. Then came the glaciers from the hills, forcing their way into these gorges, and the ice compressed and constrained, tore at the rocks and turned the ravines into their present U-shaped trenches. The typical east Wicklow glen is long and straight, an ice-eroded trench into which the tributary streams descend in cataracts, and with a marked change of level, with a waterfall in its main stream, near its head.

Of this nature are Glenmacnass and Glendalough and Glenmalure, and the hills have, too, fine lakes, either in the valleys or in corrie hollows beneath the heights. The Wicklow hills form a great barrier between the Kildare plains to the west and the narrow strip of lowland between the sea and hill to the east. The hill passes—the Sally Gap and the Wicklow Gap are high, both over the 1000 feet contour—and the recent making of the Wicklow Gap into a good road for motors has brought a real change and a new ease of communication between east and west in this area. Study of place-names suggests that the eastern lowland was settled much later than the western one.

Yet there were settlers on the hills early, there are prehistoric cairns on the Dublin hills and elsewhere, notably on Baltinglass Hill, and the bulk of the remains indicate that these early men were concentrated on the north-west of the range. It may be that they came to work the gold from the hill rivers. Tradition says the early Irish gold came from Leinster, though the first historical record is that of the finding of a 22-oz. troy nugget in 1795, and the inevitable minor gold rush that followed it. The finds were in the glens between Croghan Kinsella and Shillelagh and the lode from which they came has never been found: it is thought that the outcrop must be buried under the glacial drifts. It is possible that the Leinster streams did provide the metal

THE MILITARY ROAD

for the gold ornaments of early Ireland; equally it may have come from other places as well in the country. Lead, zinc and copper ores are also associated with the Leinster granite, they have been extensively worked in the Avoca area, east of the hills, and also in the mountain valleys themselves, particulary at Glendalough and Glenmalure. During the nineteenth century the Glendalough workings were the biggest lead mines in operation in Ireland.

The long stretches of high-level moor and the deep glens have also provided retreat and hideouts. Here came St. Kevin looking for a hermitage; here Irishmen could hold out against the English forces, and in 1798 the Wicklows were, for years after the suppression of the rising, the safe hiding-place of some of its great leaders. The Government were sufficiently alarmed by 1798 to do in Ireland what they had already done in Scotland: build a series of military roads with barracks at key-points; and this old line, running over the mountains well over the 1000-foot line now provides a fine introduction to the Leinster hills.

Dublin itself sprawls southward in a suburbia that climbs up on to the slopes of the Dublin hills in thinning clusters of houses. Out beyond Rathfarnham, in the Rockbrook area, the old military road leaves the houses behind and begins to climb rapidly out on to the mountain uplands. Behind, the city lies in its hollow fronting the wide sweep of Dublin Bay, a sparkling sea, and the sunshine glinting on roof and spire; the road, running through green fields and clustered trees, looks back upon the town framed between their trunks and branches. But the grass and trees soon give place to moorland, bog grass that shows golden in autumn, ling, dwarf gorse and all the dark tracks and turf cuttings of the townsfolk.

Gaining the main spine of the Leinster ridge, the road proceeds along it, skirting the head of Glencree (*Gleann cruidhe*, the glen of cattle) where the fields finger up into the hills and then climbing over the shoulder of Kippure (2475 feet, "the trunk of the yew tree") beneath which lie two little corrie lakes of Lough Bray, Upper and Lower, and on, past where the River Liffey rises in the peat mosses, to the Sally Gap, the gap of the willows (*bearna saileac*). It is country much like the Scottish Lammermuirs, great shoulders of hills, in autumn especially, patterned with colour, the heather and the gorse and the vivid yellow-gold of the bog grass, the green and pink of the moss. It is country, too, that is exceedingly wet and wearisome to walk after rain, like plashing through a gigantic sponge.

At the Sally Gap, a broad hollow in the heart of the range, between 1600 and 1700 feet above the sea, there is a cross-roads, the military road in rough condition keeping on straight for Glendalough, whilst on either hand good roads lead down to the east and to the west. Westward, one descends into an open valley, with attractive groups of pines, and then to Kilbride and the big reservoir of Blessington which feeds the hydro-electric scheme at Pollaphuca (*Poll a phúca*, the *púca's*— a kind of water sprite—hole). Pollaphuca, before the dam was built, was one of the many fine waterfalls of the Leinster hills —there is another famous one close to Dublin on the east side of the mountains at Powerscourt. More exciting than the west road from the Sally Gap is that to the east, which runs high on the mountainside, looking down into the sudden rift of the valley below in which lies Lough Luggala (*Loch Lug a' lagha*, the lake of the hollow of the hill). Round its head the hillside rises in sheer cliffs, with trees clinging to their foot; the head of the lake hid amongst these heights is a small green haugh edged with a yellow strand of sand. Descending to the lake the hill streams come cascading in brown, peat-stained torrents, whilst above are the rolling lines of the hill-ridges with the clouds sailing swiftly across the wide horizons.

It is of course Glendalough (*Gleann da locha*, the valley of the two lakes) that draws the crowds, Glendalough of St. Kevin and the clustered churches and round tower (33). The old pilgrim road to it crossed the Wicklows by the second great pass to the south-west of the Sally Gap, the Wicklow Gap, and that perhaps is the right way to approach the valley. For it seems it is the way that St. Kevin (Coemgan in Irish spelling, died 618 or 622) came too, when he went looking for a hermitage for prayer and penance.

Coming from the west, then, you pass through the village of Hollywood, remembering the story of how the saint went through thick woods, with an angel to clear the way for him, and how he blessed the trees, so that the right name would seem to be Holy and not Holly, wood. As the road begins to climb you look into a rocky defile running parallel with the hillside,

GLENDALOUGH

an old marginal drainage channel of the Glacial period cut by water dammed against the hill-ridge by ice sheets on the lower ground. There is another very fine cut of the same sort east of the hills, at the Scalp, on the road between Dublin and Enniskerry. As the road climbs into the open valley of the Gap the plains lie spread behind, and the mountains themselves are a dapple of rock and grass, heather and bracken, with the velvet brown of the turf cuttings. The watershed is crossed at about 1600 feet, and with it there is that immediate change, the sudden alteration from the broad western glen to the narrow eastern one. Beneath a crag is the corrie lake of Nahanagan, the glen is pocked with old lead workings, and there is a sudden descent, the stream pouring down in cascades, to the trenched glen below, the valley of Glendasan, which joins with the foot of Glendalough, so that of a sudden you see the round tower and the woods that cling to the steep rocks above the old monastic settlement.

Kevin went right up the glen, past the lower lake to the cliff-circled one above it, and made his hermitage in a cave on one of the cliffs above the water. Earlier, that cave had been used as a burial-place by the Megalithic people, just as they were able to use Kelly's Cave at Cong, instead of constructing a special cairn. Now Kevin settled in it, but very soon he was joined by other disciples, and the community overflowed to the foot of the upper lake. Glendalough rapidly became famous and increased so much in size that it required a second move to a wider space down the valley—where now stands the round tower and the massive gateway of the old Celtic monastery. So Oengus the Culdee (*c.* 800) speaks of "multitudinous Glendalough", the "cemetery of the west of the world". And an Irish life of the saint, written in verse, speaks of the valley as:

> A glen without threshing floor or corn rick,
> Only rugged rocks above it,
> (Yet) a glen where no one is refused entertainment,
> (For) the grace of the Lord is there.

It is said that the soil of the burial-ground of Glendalough was hallowed by bringing earth from Rome to it, and to go seven times there was equivalent to doing the pilgrimage to Rome. It continued to be a great place of pilgrimage, even after attacks on the pilgrims during the post-Reformation Penal legislation against such gatherings: in 1714 the sheriff reported, for instance, how he had had word of "a riotous assembly from all parts of the kingdom, at the seven churches, contrary to Act of Parliament, in order to pay a superstitious worship to St. Kevin". The account goes on to tell how the official party pulled down the pilgrims' tents, "threw down and demolished their superstitious crosses, filled up and destroyed their wells, and apprehended and committed one, Toole, a Popish schoolmaster".

St. Kevin's Glendalough has about it today a sense of quiet and peace hanging over the ruined churches and carved crosses. It is probably the most beautiful of the Wicklow valleys, showing to perfection their blend of lake and rock and woodland hidden in the defile trenched in the more open moors above them. I would put in a plea for seeing Glendalough and all these valleys very early in the spring, or late winter, when the moors are still vivid with the dead bracken and the leafless twigs of the woods are running with the sap. They climb up the steep slopes, these woods, partly now forestry plantation, partly older woodland, and there are against the brackens and the dark needles of the pines, the larch woods and the oaks. The oak twigs take upon themselves early in spring a smoky tinge, like a faint haze from a wood fire over the hillside, whilst the larch twigs are a rich yellow. Here in the Wicklows are two kinds of larch, the ordinary yellow-twigged European sort, and the Japanese, which has a kind of violet-russet coloured branch; the two in the plantations are complementary, setting one another off.

From Glendalough one can rejoin the old military road and climb up over the ridge which separates that valley from Glenmalure (*Gleann maoilúghra*). Behind, as you snake through the woods, you look over the eastern strip between mountain and sea, and to the isolated Sugarloaf hills at Bray. And then there is a viciously steep descent to Glenmalure, beside a stream which comes roaring down through a wood in cataracts. Below is the level floor of the valley, the old shell of the barracks of Drumgoff and the military road climbing away beyond them to Aghavannagh at the south end of the Wicklow range. Up the valley there is a good road as far as the ford at Barravore, woodlands again, small farms

31 Lugnaquillia and Glenmalure, Co. Wicklow

32 The Slieve Mish and the hill fort of Caherconree, Co. Kerry

33 Glendalough, Co. Wicklow

34 Mount Brandon, Co. Kerry

and fields in the flat of the glen, the streams falling in waterfalls from the cliffs above, and the scars of the abandoned lead mines.

At Barravore the road fades into a track, growing fainter and wetter as you ascend. All this country is being quickly planted and eventually the forest will extend almost to the main summit of the Wicklow hills. I walked up to the watershed ridge overlooking Glen Imail on the west of the ridge, passing young trees earthed up in trenches waiting to plant, and new fences lately put up. There is a sudden steep, with waterfalls, and then a long pull over the upper part of the hollow, a broad saucer of peat hag and morass, sodden and sticky in wintertime and barely holding the trace of the track. You look back to the trenched valley below, perhaps with mist curling over it, so that the sudden descent to the rock-bound glen looks like the jaws of hell in some Irish vision story of the underworld. Round about the broad and easy heather slopes, or the grass and rush of the bogs, waiting for the young trees to be set in them; below that fantastic rift of Glenmalure (31).

The summit is reached at 2283 feet and the descent to the broad open Glen of Imail, entirely different from Glenmalure, spacious and airy, with woods and roads edged with birches that set off the outlook to the circling hills. At the summit is a notice of An Oige, the Irish Youth Hostels, pointing the skyline walk from Dublin to Lugnaquillia (3039 feet, the highest top in Ireland outside of Kerry). Its name on this board is given as *Lug na coille*, the hollow of the wood, which in view of both ancient and modern afforestation in the area seems reasonable enough, though the name is more often explained as *Lug na gcoileach*, the hollow of the cocks (grouse). It can be readily ascended from either side, either by climbing out of Glenmalure and then walking up a spur, or by following a brawling stream from Coan in Glen Imail up beside the boundary of the military range there. In the latter glen the River Slaney takes its origin, too, from the slopes of Lug.

It is interesting to realise that not all the cover of altered sedimentary rock is gone from the Wicklow granite crest: patches remain, apparently not the real old roof but pendants from it which were greatly altered by the igneous rock, and that it is these that form the high ground to which you look up from Glen Imail, the top of Lugnaquillia and of Table Mountain, and that it is the granite which floors the cols between them.

Glenmalure and Glen Imail are closely linked with the events both of Red Hugh's dramatic escape, and with the 1798 rising. It is becoming an annual event now, at Christmas time, for an energetic party to set off across the hills from Dublin for Glenmalure, in recapitulation of the O'Donnell's historic flight.

Something of O'Neill and O'Donnell has already been told. What must be realised is that the first invasion from England of the Anglo-Normans was eventually stabilised—the English in the Pale round Dublin; others of them absorbed into Irish life, more Irish than the Irish themselves. The Tudor period was a reconquest of Ireland, a reconquest of large areas which had continued to live under Irish (Brehon) law and customs, and in which Irish poetry and literature continued to flourish under the patronage of the great lords. The Tudor attack was two-pronged: it aimed to destroy the Catholic faith of the Irish in the name of the Reformation, and to destroy the Irish way of life and make Ireland another England. The stand made by Hugh O'Neill, the great Ulster leader, and his able second, Red Hugh O'Donnell, and which ended in defeat at Kinsale, meant the end of these large areas of continuing Irish life. The policy of eviction of the native owners and plantation by incomers was effected everywhere but in the wildest parts of the country. The fight would go on, and in the end be successful, but the Tudor reconquest broke the developing continuity of Irish Gaeldom: the Celtic civilisation that should have extended into the present day, adapting itself to each new circumstance, was shattered, and modern Ireland is faced with the problem of rediscovering her heritage and integrating it into her daily life.

Red Hugh, who was born in 1572, was a natural leader of his people, and the Government accordingly decided to kidnap him. In 1587 they sent a ship to Donegal which pretended to be from Spain and intent on trade. Hugh was got aboard and the old trick worked of making him drunk at a party and setting sail for Dublin and prison. There he remained until the Christmas of 1591, when he and some others managed to escape via a privy and set off over the hills to Glenmalure, in whose recesses was the stronghold of Fiach Mac Hugh, a sure friend. The two sons of Shane O'Neill came with Hugh, Henry O'Neill got lost in the

1798

dark and Art died of exposure sheltering in a snowstorm under a rock. Meantime, another of the party reached Glenmalure and a rescue party with food and drink set off. They were in time to save Hugh O'Donnell, though he suffered frostbite and the loss of his two big toes.

The rising began with enormous successes, like the victory of the Yellow Ford in 1598 and that of the Curlews, the next year, the last that the Irish would win. Spanish help was looked for and eventually came, too little, and in the wrong place: to Kinsale, already in a country largely subdued, instead of sailing to a safe port in the north or west. O'Neill and O'Donnell went south and on December 24th, 1601, apparently because of Hugh's rash determination to fight at once, were defeated.

Seventeen ninety-eight is a different story. The country was restive under a corrupt Parliament, the refusal of full Catholic emancipation by the tiny Protestant ascendancy, and then a savage Insurrection Act, which gave the Lord-Lieutenant power, in 1796, to proclaim any area under military law. The Habeas Corpus Act was suspended, and the Government troops were let loose to do as they would. Meantime, republican ideas of freedom were in the air, and the Kildare-born Wolfe Tone, imbued with them. He began his work through the ordinary channels, only planning a rising when these failed.

Round the Wicklow mountains the British troops were occupied, before the rising, in a riot of torture and terrorism— of which an account by a contemporary, a Carmelite lay brother, Luke Cullen, reads only too like events of modern times in Nazi- and Soviet-occupied countries. The troops' behaviour was admitted by their leaders; Sir Ralph Abercrombie, who was in command of them for a short time before the rising, reported that the army was "in such a state of licentiousness as must render it formidable to everyone but the enemy".

It is against this background that you must see the 1798 memorials in all the towns and villages beneath the Wicklow hills. The rising began on May 24th, 1798, and affected Ulster, Meath and Leinster, the only really serious threat coming from Wexford. Inevitably it failed, and some of its leaders, like the gallant Michael O'Dwyer, took to the hills. Michael O'Dwyer and Hugh O'Donnell are both commemorated in the Irish inscription on a great boulder of granite beside the road up

Glenmalure. There, and over in Glen Imail, Michael was able to elude capture for five years before eventually surrendering on terms. In Glen Imail the cottage at Derrynamuck is preserved in which he and his companions were surprised in February 1799. The soldiers burned the house, and one of O'Dwyer's party, Samuel MacAllister, who was wounded, saved the others by going to the door and drawing all the troops' fire and attention on himself.

South from Lugnaquillia the continuous mountain line comes to an end in a scatter of lesser hills between which several main roads carry the traffic from east to west. Then, at Newtownbarry, the real mountains begin again, extending from Mount Leinster (2610 feet) south toward New Ross. These are the Blackstairs mountains, crossed only by the Scullogue Gap (*scológ*, a small farmer) at 600 feet.

They are mountains most satisfying to the eye. If you come south through the rich wooded country from Castledermot, Mount Leinster, showing as a graceful smooth-shouldered mountain ahead, dominates the scene, whilst by the road, in spring, there are orchards in a flush of pink blossom. From Newtownbarry there is a small mountainy gated-road which climbs up and over the shoulder of Mount Leinster and down to Borris in the west, by forestry plantation and open moor and all the plain laid out beneath the sudden rise of the ridge. The crest of this little road is called the Nine Stones, and there are nine small cairns set by the track by someone, though the original of the name, perhaps a Megalithic monument, seems lost to sight. Mount Leinster is a smooth and rounded height, but southward the lower ridges show some hackles of granite tors and the Scullogue Gap is littered with grey boulder beds. Below, the River Barrow runs in a deep trench, and across it is the isolated and shapely mass of Brandon Hill (1694 feet).

It is not country ruggedly dramatic, this of the Barrow and the Blackstairs; rather of green woods and fields, a broad river still carrying some barge traffic, and beyond it the massive line of the hills. Yet it has about it a beauty all its own, and a Barrow man will wonder what the crowds can see in Killarney.

Connected with the goodness of the land and the communication line formed by the Barrow are a series of important Celtic church foundations, which form, as it were, a kind of western

THE BLACKSTAIRS MOUNTAINS

border to the Leinster chain. Most were in sympathy with, or of, the Culdee reform movement of the late eighth to early ninth centuries, and were also centres at which the art of the High Cross began to be highly developed. You can list these old sites from St. Mullins and Graiguenamanagh on the Barrow, on by Castledermot and Moone and Kilcullen (at all of which are fine High Crosses, carved in the rough granite and with a certain massive simplicity about them), and finally to Tallaght of St. Maelruain on the outskirts of Dublin.

With that line of old churches and crosses set beneath the mountains one can come back to Dublin, and yet another aspect of the Leinster hills—the way in which they are a kind of background to the city, and in which they frame the southern half of the bay, so that the seaward approach to the port, the city with the Wicklow hills on the one side and the lesser headland of Howth upon the other, is claimed as one of the loveliest in Europe.

CHAPTER VII

The Kingdom of Mourne

It was in Mourne that I saw the Brocken spectre. It was a cold day early in February, snow had fallen overnight and dusted the countryside with white powder and the car slid and skidded on the bends. When I left it beside Clonachullion Hill and began to follow the old track up beside the Trassey River to the Hare's Gap the puddles were all surfaced with cat ice, whilst the mist still drifted on the heights, with sunlit gaps and patches rending it here and there. It is a long steady walk up the glen—the Brandy Pad is the name of the track through the gap above, for this is smugglers' country—and as I got higher, under the final rise to the rectangular cut in the main line of the Mourne mountains, that is the pass of the Hare, the mist thickened and it began to snow slightly.

On the crest of the pass the sun came through again, so that I could see the High Mournes round me, with the cloud still on their heights. Beside me, in a steep ascent over heather with runs of rock, rose the 2394 feet of Slieve Bearnagh (the gapped mountain), with the great boundary wall of the Belfast Water Commissioners heading straight for its summit. I turned up beside this wall, the snow lying in the joints of the granite outcrops in fantastic hieroglyphs, and piled against the wall in a long drift. Higher, it was plastered in a thin frozen cover over the hillside, up which one kicked a route. The summit of the mountain is formed of ragged torrs of granite, of which there are two groups separated by a col, hence probably the name of the gapped mountain. I came out on the first of these as the mist came down thicker, so that I could see nothing but the fangs of rock beside me and the cloud driven by a biting wind moving past them.

Above, the sun seemed to be dispersing the mist, and it came through in hesitant fashion, so that I, leaning over the wall, could look down through gaps in the cloud to the sunlit fields of Co. Down, cleared of the morning's snow now and shaded in pastel greens with a blue lake sparkling. But before that fuller clearing came, I looked across the glen below the ridge of Bearnagh to the opposite slopes of Slieve Meel-More (*Sliabh mael mor*, the big bare mountain), all veiled in the cloud. On that cloud I first saw a small circular rainbow, and then with the sun gaining strength, at my back, the full Broken spectre: myself leaning on the wall encircled by concentric rainbows and projected across the valley on to the wall of mist. This is the famous spectre named from the Brocken in Germany from which it was first described, the magnified shadow flung across a deep valley. The rainbows, "glories", only appear when the light is fairly bright. When a group of climbers sees the spectre, whilst each climber see the shadows of all, the halo only encircles his own head. Each, then, somewhat invidiously, sees himself with a rainbow and his companions in mere black and white!

The clouds cleared and I stood looking west, along the broad rounded curve of the Mourne ridge, to Slieve Commedagh (*Sliabh coimhéada*, the mountain of the watching, 2512 feet) and to Slieve Donard (*Sliabh Domhanghairt*, St. Donard's Mountain, 2796 feet), the highest point of the hills. The waterworks boundary wall marched along their crest, and Donard rose in a great round molehill shape, all plastered and glittering with snow.

These Mourne mountains, a slender line extending for some fourteen or fifteen miles from Newcastle in the north to Rostrevor south-west of it, and all in Co. Down, are one of the most striking of the Irish groups of hills (36). The attraction lies in the line of peaks, from the rounded Donard, by the torrs of Slieve Bearnagh and Slieve Binnian (variously given on the maps as Bignian and Bingian, *Sliabh binneann*, mountain of the sharp peak, 2249 feet), by the cleft of the Spelga Pass, and then by the green and rounded heights above Rostrevor to the sudden descent to the blue water of Carlingford Lough. From wherever you see them, north or south, from Slieve Croob, or Saul of St. Patrick, or from Carlingford, the line maintains its shapely symmetry, its splendid upspringing from the lowland and the sea.

It is granite country. On the low ground there is the Newry granite, extending roughly from that town north to Slieve Croob, of Caledonian Age like that of the Leinster hills. The Mourne granites, however, belong to the Tertiary intrusions, and to see them in perspective means a map of Scotland as well as Ireland, and with a thought for Iceland as well. World-wide mountain-building movements in this period of geological time built up the great mountain chains of the present day, the Alps, Himalayas, Rockies, Andes, to mention some of them. That great orogen did not build fresh mountain chains in Ireland, though it may have steepened some existing folds. But in the north, in northern Ireland and western Scotland, the Tertiary epoch was one of great igneous activity, outpouring of great sheets of basalt lava, now represented in the Antrim hills, in the Giant's Causeway and Fingal's Cave in the island of Staffa, and in the terraced hills of Lorne and Mull in Scotland. At a deeper level there were vast intrusions of coarse-grained igneous rocks, acid granites and basic gabbros, and these intrusions, now exposed by erosion, have a marked concentric arrangement with the different rocks in circling rings (technically, cone sheets and ring dykes). You may see this structure set out like a diagram at Ardnamurchan in Scotland, or from Slieve Gullion above Newry in a somewhat less dramatic fashion.

And naming these great centres of igneous activity is to link up mountain and island in an exciting litany, Mull and Rum and Eigg, the Cuillin of Skye, St. Kilda, Arran, and in Ireland, Barnesmore in Donegal, and in the north-east, Carlingford, Slieve Gullion and the Mourne mountains. It is thought that the Slieve Gullion centre was the oldest of these three closely associated centres; that Carlingford came next, its rugged gabbro perhaps of the same age as that of the Cuillin of Skye; and Mourne last. Four different kinds of granite have been distinguished in Mourne; the process was one of successive intrusions, and the whole outcrop covers fifty-five square miles, the largest one of Tertiary granite in Britain or Ireland.

Granite, then, is the theme of Mourne, forming the higher hills and contrasting with the gentler, green slopes of the sedimentary rocks into which it was intruded and which form the heights above Carlingford Lough at Rostrevor. Granite quarries pit the mountain-sides, and the clink of hammers still rings out on the

35 The eastern cliffs under the summit of Mount Brandon, Co. Kerry

36 The M

of Mourne

37 The Upper Lake and Macgillycuddy Reeks, Killarney

38 The Silent Valley reservoir in the Mourne Mountains, Co. Down

still air. There is a long history of granite working in Mourne: it began with improving transport at the end of the eighteenth century, helped by the closeness of the hills to the sea and the little ports, and it started with small groups of workers. Their huts, rough structures of stone, with the stone troughs in which they tempered the tools of their trade, are everywhere to be seen. The peak came in the middle of the nineteenth century and mitigated the effects of the famine in this area: stone was worked not only for Belfast, but for the English market and Mourne claims to have "paved Lancashire". The returning "stone" boats brought loads of Welsh slates to replace the traditional thatch. After the Second World War there came a fresh interest in Mourne granite, both for constructional purposes and for tombstones, and several large quarries were opened.

The Caledonian Newry granite has also been much used for building purposes, as also that of the Wicklow hills to the south, which last provided material for many Dublin buildings and also for the Thames Embankment in London.

There is a fascination over this quarry work, the ring of hammers on the mountain-side, the ports and the small sailing boats, and the smoke-stained streets of the industrial towns of England, which seem so far remote from Mourne and the sea.

One must see Mourne, then, as a curving line of hills, at two points literally sweeping down into the sea, at Newcastle and Rostrevor, and in the corner of land between these points, south-east of the hills, the gently sloped triangle of land that is the kingdom of Mourne. Of this enclosed and isolated farmland below the hills Prof. Estyn Evans has remarked that there is nowhere else in Ireland an area so densely populated and so isolated (and the same writer is responsible for a detailed study of Mourne, the only one so far of an Irish mountain area).[*] It was an area known to the early settlers, the Megalithic people coming in by sea, and their great cairns are to be seen over the whole district; but it may well have been conservative thereafter, clinging to its Megalithic traditions long after things had changed in the rest of Ireland. The Anglo-Normans did not penetrate into it, maintaining castles at the two narrow entries at Newcastle and Rostrevor, and a toehold at Greencastle, on

[*] *Mourne Country*, Dundalk, 1951.

the point opposite their town of Carlingford. Irish customs survived here, and the last native Irish speakers are only lately dead.

The old name was the *Beanna Boirche* the mountains of Boirche, an individual said to have ruled his kingdom from Slieve Binnian, herding his flocks upon the hillsides. In the thirteenth century, about the same time as the Anglo-Norman invasion, the MacMahons moved into this country and took possession of it, and the corruption of their family name gave us Mourne.

Here then was a typical hillslope community, with booleys on the hills (the Mourne name for booleying is *creaghting*) and with the sea below for fish and to supply the fields with wrack for fertiliser; later to be the export route for granite, and the import one for smuggled goods. Seaweed is still cultivated for use on the land—by placing stones in beds on the muddy flats of Mill Bay on which the wrack can grow and then be conveniently cut when required.

You can seize on the essential shape of Mourne best from a distance. From the nose of the Carlingford peninsula, from Ballagan Point, you stand upon a grey shingle beach and look across a sea sparkling and blue to the emerald fields of Greencastle and the undulating triangle of Mourne, with at its back the whole line of the hills from Rostrevor to Donard. I saw it with the heights glittering with snow and the lowland in contrast brown and green, with the central dark lump of Knockchree (1013 feet, the mountain of the heart, apparently because a certain MacCremon, dying abroad in the Low Countries, asked for his heart to be brought home and buried here). The mountains were white, sparkling, and you could see the way in which the Mourne fields climbed up their slopes to a level of some 600 feet.

Or else you can climb up Slieve Binnian and sit in the sunshine high above the granite quarries, on the pink granite boulder beds all grown with bushy blaeberries, and look down on Mourne, with the fields flowing away from the rough pastures down to the sea. Again, Knockchree rises centrally, but now there is the prospect across the fiord of Carlingford to the ragged crest of Carlingford Mountain. And there is the sea—perhaps that is the most impressive part of the Mourne outlook, that wide horizon of ocean, so long that the skyline shows the curved roundness of the earth.

Two roads cross the Mournes: from Hilltown to Rostrevor and from Hilltown to Kilkeel. That last is the Spelga Pass and a real mountain road through the heart of the hills. West of it the Pigeon Rock Mountain shows the contact of granite with sediment, and east of it are the real High Mournes, leading up to the culmination of Donard. The road runs through a boggy flat cradled high in the hills, an old booley site, by name the Deer's Meadow. The name recalls some of the past animal life of these hills. As well as the deer, the buzzard was to be seen and the hen harrier. The latter is said to have nested near Rostrevor at the end of last century, and the golden and white-tailed eagles were also still nesting here up to about 1840.

The Deer's Meadow is now being turned into a reservoir for Belfast. The Mourne glens are bleak, and a flooded Deer's Meadow seems likely to add to their beauty, just as the reservoir in the Silent Valley has done. The latter, a narrow glen leading up to Slieve Bearnagh, and with Slieve Binnian's torrs on the one side of its mouth, has, by its flooding, turned into a beautiful highland-looking lake (38). The work was begun in 1923, but not completed until 1933. In addition there are more recent works and some still in progress. A beautiful park-like entry has been constructed, short mown grass with a variety of shrubs in striking contrast to the heather moors above, and this brings one to the great dam and the blue water of the reservoir. Round about, the most rugged of the Mourne hills rise steeply, their crests lifting from a very marked high peneplain level, on the flat of which lies Lough Shannagh (*Loch Sionnach*, the lake of the foxes), the largest natural lake in these hills.

Mourne water, off granite and peat, is soft and pure. The River Bann rises in the Deer's Meadow, and its water is famous for bleaching linen. To mark off the gathering ground for the Belfast reservoir in Silent Valley, the great wall in drystone was built, which marches over all the High Mourne summits. Something in Mourne, then, keeps one in touch with the lowland, the granite workings, the reservoirs and this tremendous wall: the mountains lack the wilderness they once had, and it is hardly possible to get lost with that great wall for guide along the crests.

Knockshee (*Cnoc sidhe*, the fairy hill, 1144 feet) is a good point from which to see the lower, grassy Mournes. It has the typical conical *síd* shape and a steep walk over short turf brings one to the summit and a round Bronze Age cairn, apparently undisturbed except for the building of a small marker cairn on top of it. Round about, the hills are rounded and grassy with patches of bracken, and the valleys open, with settlements running far up them. And from Rostrevor and Warrenpoint, the forestry plantations ascend to the tops of the ridges. It is country like much of the Scottish borderland, and in the clipped speech of the people you will often be reminded of that same country: after all there was much plantation and settlement from Scotland. Immediately below Knockshee is a large dolmen, the denuded core of a Megalithic cairn; beyond one looks to Greencastle and Carlingford. Greencastle used to have a famous sheep fair. Just as under the Killarney hills, at Killorglin, the goat fair included the enthroning of a champion goat to preside over the market, so here a ram was enthroned on the castle walls. Greencastle Ram Fair is no longer in being, but Killorglin "Puck" Fair is not only active but has become a tourist attraction.

Inevitably, it is to Donard that one turns. It is a great rounded heap of a hill, bare and smooth (36). There is contrast here in Mourne; it is the lower rocky tops that allow plant life to thrive best in the shelter of the crags; smooth windswept uplands like Donard are inhibiting to growth. It is a bare hill, with short heather, moss and club moss on it and runs of bouldery scree. It dominates Mourne, how much one does not realise until it is seen from far off, from Slieve Gullion, for instance, when the dome seems almost isolated from the other peaks.

Here St. Donard took possession of two Megalithic chambered cairns, one on the summit (now ruined by the operations of the surveyors making the Ordnance maps, and later by the wall builders), and one on the shoulder overlooking the old sandhill habitation sites of Newcaste. In them St. Donard, who is said to have been a convert of St. Patrick, and to have died March 24th, 506, established a hermitage and oratory. Below, on the plain, near Newcastle, was his principal church, Maghera, placed within an older *rath* or *cashel* whose stone walls still circle the shell of the old church. Outside is the stump of a round tower, and from this point too there is a magnificent prospect of Donard and

Slieve Commedagh. A mountain pilgrimage long followed Donard to the top of the mountain, and a beautiful tradition tells how the saint continues to say Mass each Sunday at the cairn.

I like O'Donovan's account of his ascent, given in his Ordnance Survey letters of 1834; how he went with intent "to wash off in St. Domangard's Well the many sins I had committed by cursing dogs, ganders, over-inquisitive people and petty country landlords". And then, over the scree of the final rise, which is steep: "Up this steep and rocky passage I skipped from stone to stone with the agility of a goat, but was obliged to wait for my guide whom age had rendered less vigorous."

It is easy enough to climb Donard. First through the woods of Donard Lodge, with the Glen River crystal clear cascading over rocks. As you go higher, the pines and rhododendrons frame the view back to Newcastle, with its strand, sandhills and blue sea. Above the woods there is a broad open valley leading up to the col between Slieve Donard and Slieve Commedagh, with a rough track along the floor. On either hand are crags: the massive Eagle's Rock which forms a spur of Donard and less prominent ones on the Commedagh—Shan Slieve (old mountain) ridge. Steeply up from the valley head to the col and then still more steeply to Donard summit and the ruined cairn.

I went up in a gale of wind, and with a long wreath of snow on the north side of the great wall. Small snow showers marched over the Mourne heights, veiling them in thinnest lace. The sea was intensely blue, contrasting with the moors and the small fields, the woodland and pasture. I fought the wind up the glen to the col, thrown back on my heels now and again, and on Donard summit, faced it on the return, a gale so violent that at first I could make no progress against it downhill and saw myself, like Donard, a hermit on the heights.

In clear weather the outlook from Slieve Donard is not merely over the Mourne mountains to Carlingford and Slieve Gullion, or along the coast, or inland over Co. Down and beyond. It includes the Isle of Man, the Cumberland mountains, Arran in Scotland and Snowdon in Wales. The old name, before Donard came, was Slieve Slainge (another personal name) or Benn Boirche and it is not surprising to find it in the Triads of Ireland —The Three Heights of Ireland: Croagh Patrick, Ae Chualann (either Lugnaquillia or the Great Sugarloaf near Bray), Benn Boirche. (These Triads are a literary form: you find similar numerical groupings in the Bible, and they were very popular in Celtic Ireland. A good Triad should have a twist in it: "Three cold things that seethe; a well, the sea, new ale.")

On the farther side of the col linking Slieve Donard and Slieve Commedagh, where the path from the Hare's Gap comes over the hills, are the castles of Commedagh, where the granite is weathered into a group of pinnacles and torrs: and near by is one of the localities for seeking good crystals of quartz, beryl, topaz, tourmaline and so on, which occur in the Mourne granites. In fact this particular spot is called the Diamond Rocks because of the sparkling quartz (rock crystal) and the like to be got there. These Diamond Rocks are on the slopes of the mountain between the castles and the Hare's Gap.

If you leave the Mournes and cross the undulating drumlin country of Co. Down over to the lesser heights of Slieve Croob (1755 feet) you may ascend to the cromlech of Legananny, which is not only a striking enough looking Megalith in itself, but is most dramatically situated. It sits upon the crest of the shoulder of the mountain Cratlieve (1417 feet), a tripod supporting an enormous capstone, and from it the outlook is across the lowland to the whole northern line of the Mourne mountains. I saw them from there late in the evening, when the sun was low in the west, and the mountain line all white with snow, glistening frostily in the still cold air. Legananny is the kind of site these Megalithic builders seem to have loved, upland with the land spread out below and a far-ranging outlook to the distant hills.

Westward lies Newry (*Iubhar cinn tragha*, the yew at the head of the strand) on the border between counties Down and Armagh, and beyond it is the isolated mass of Slieve Gullion (*Sliabh cuilinn*, the mountain of the holly). It is a long heathery ridge, rising to 1894 feet with lesser heights about it, the rugged little ridges of Forkill and the broad-shouldered swell of Cam Lough Mountain, with a blue lake between it and Slieve Gullion foot. From the cairn on the top you look down on these ringing lesser heights, and a geological map of the area will come to life, for these hills mark the outcrops of the harder igneous rocks of the complex of which Slieve Gullion itself forms the centre (25).

The cairn upon the top is a passage grave, with the roof of the central chamber fallen in, so that you can see the way it was built, of huge slabs, beehive style, and the passage leading into it. Some way off, on the hilltop, which is broad and hummocky with boggy patches, is a small lake, said to bleach linen whiter than any other water in Ireland. Not unnaturally the swelling ridge of Slieve Gullion, with the cairn and the surprising lakelet on its top, has attracted a good number of legends and traditions round itself. Here is one of the places where the Finn story has an important localisation, for instance. It is the old theme of the hero winning wisdom from the *sid*, or Otherworld, Slieve Gullion here being regarded as a fairy mound. Finn bathed in the lake and was turned into a feeble old man. The Fianna then attacked the *sid* and its lord came out and gave Finn to drink from a golden cup, which not only restored him but gave him the gift of supernatural wisdom. This same story is also attached to a site at Limerick, Cahernarny. In another version Finn's wisdom, which was localised in his thumb which he accordingly used to suck, is explained by his having had his hand caught in the door of the *sid* slammed to against his entry, and it is this version that is attached to Slievenamon in Co. Tipperary.

All this country is linked with real history too. It is the way into Ulster, the road on through the Gap of the North, and it is odd to reflect that Ulster, protected by hill and marsh and lake and wood, was once the great stronghold of Irish national feeling and resistance. Plantation and settlement have turned much of it into the very reverse of what it once was.

This country of Armagh is linked with the name of the great Archbishop of Armagh, the martyr Blessed Oliver Plunket. Amongst these hills and fields he served his people and eluded arrest for a considerable period. Here too was the hide-out of the so-called Irish Robin Hood, Redmond O'Hanlon, a contemporary of Blessed Oliver. This Rob Roy of Ireland was, like many Irish "Torys" and "Rapparees", of good birth and breeding, forced out on to the hill by eviction and seizure of his property. Blessed Oliver is said to have visited many of these displaced Irishmen and persuaded them to emigrate rather than live "on their keeping" in the Ulster hills. Redmond, supported by a company of like-minded men, managed to survive some twenty years before he was eventually killed by treachery. Many stories are told of his gallantry and dash, including one of how he got much-needed horses and equipment for his men—by posing as a peaceable citizen and requesting an armed escort home. The escort he led into an ambush, and the surprised soldiers were disarmed and sent to walk back to their barracks.

On the slopes of Slieve Gullion is the early Celtic church site of Killeevy (*Cell Sléibhe Cuilinn*, the church of the holly mountain). It was founded by St. Monenna (died 517) and was one of the most important early Irish nunneries. There remain at the site two churches built one on to the other, end to end. The eastmost has a fourteenth-century east window decorated outside with two carved human heads; the west church has an Irish Romanesque window of eleventh- or twelfth-century date, and its main doorway apparently incorporates material from an even older structure, perhaps eighth or ninth century. This earliest church had the typical Irish Celtic doorway with a huge lintel stone, here still in place, a block of granite estimated to weigh some ten tons. The Megalithic tradition of building in big stones seems to have been a very persistent one!

There is a holy well on the slopes above, with a setting and cross put up in 1929. Meantime over in the glen above Rostrevor is another interesting Celtic site, of St. Bronach, with a well dedicated to St. Brigit, two early crosses, and a Celtic bell now used as the Mass bell in Rostrevor Church.

The third mountain area of this part of Ireland is the Carlingford peninsula, where the igneous rocks rise steeply from the softer sediments, the gabbro forming a rough and rugged skyline and the granite the smoother slopes. Again, this difference in the way the rocks weather shows up, on the actual hillside, the pattern of the underlying geological structure.

It is perhaps the loveliest end of Mourne, the fiord of Carlingford Lough dividing the steep slopes of Mourne from those of Carlingford, each descending in a sudden sweep to the water's edge and each tree-clad, plantations of pine and the two sorts of larch. There are most brilliant effects of light and shade here early in the morning when the colours are pale but bright, or late in the evening when they are equally vivid but of a great depth and richness.

CARLINGFORD MOUNTAIN

All this is country historic and legendary, this is the peninsula of the *Táin Bó Cuailgne*, and in the rugged line of the gabbro of Slieve Foye (1935 feet, Carlingford Mountain) the imaginative can see a petrified Finn, exhausted from throwing the large glacial erratic of Cloughmore at a rival giant on the Mournes. Carlingford was a Norse settlement, hence the *fiord* name, and later an Anglo-Norman one. In the little town are the well-preserved ruins of two castles, King John's, by the harbour, on a rock looking across the fiord to the Kingdom of Mourne and the mountains, a structure massive and grown with yellow wallflowers and valerian. Out on the low-lying farmlands of the nose of the peninsula is a place called Templetown, with a small church set on a mound, said to have belonged to the Knights Templars.

From there you can drive up a road through the heart of the mountains, a deep valley following a line of faulting or breakage in the rocks, and with the gabbros of Slieve Foye in a fantastic pattern of littered rock and craglet above you. The road climbs up to the narrow Windy Gap and then descends to Carlingford Lough more rapidly than it climbed up from the south; there is at this gap a hollow in the hills, with a boggy lake in it, and a story attached to the place. Here is the Long Woman's Grave. The tale is of two sons at their father's deathbed, the elder promising there to give the younger a fair share of the estates. He said he would take him up to a high place in the mountain and give him all he could see. So he did, but the place was this hollow at Windy Gap, where if you look round you see nothing but the immediate hillside rising on all hands. The younger son took to trading for a living and eventually loved and won a Spanish beauty, to whom he told the same tale. He brought her home and took her up to Windy Gap to show her his estates; the shock of being taken in killed her on the spot. She was very tall, according to the story, so explaining the name of the Long Woman's Grave.

A brief scramble out of this hollow puts one on the ridge of Slieve Foye and the prospect of Carlingford Lough sparkling below; the little farms fingering up the slopes of the hills on either hand, the woods, the Mourne ridges, and inland, up to Newry and the fields spreading in a checkered pattern over all the undulating ridges of Down and Armagh. Here indeed the mountains both of Mourne and Carlingford sweep down to the gentian sea in a dramatic steepness. The road, on either side, runs on the narrow space between hill and shore. It is the Irish combination of mountain and sea in its most intense and vivid expression.

CHAPTER VIII

Galtee and Comeragh

In the south, in counties Cork and Tipperary and Waterford, the mountains rise without foothills from the plains. They are of sandstone, and show the east-west trends of the Amorican movements which crumpled the Old Red and Carboniferous rocks into a series of folds, of which the crests still stand up as hills of the harder, older rock, whilst the softer Carboniferous forms the valley and plain below, the troughs of the old fold system.

Elsewhere in Ireland the variety of hill shape varies with the kind of rock, but here, in the ranges of Galtee, Knockmealdown and Comeragh, the same rock builds different sorts of hills, each group with its own individuality.

They are indeed alike in sharing that sudden rise from the plain. Round the foot of all these hills is good farmland, on the one side of the Galtees, the best in Ireland, so it is often said, the Golden Vale of Tipperary, and the grazing lands and farms of Mitchelstown on the other. There are indeed small mountainy farms on the very foot of the hills themselves and in their valleys, but below, the main roads lead through the best of level plains, and the outlook from the heights reflects this, with what is probably the most striking example of the checkerboard pattern of the Irish countryside. The climber looks down on a network of fields, criss-crossed with roads, with houses dotted here and there, or clotted into village and town. In spring the fields have gilded edges with the gorse in flower in their hedges. Their pattern is most various, changing with the season, green pasture, the darker ridges of potatoes, the glossy leaves of sugar-beet or swede or mangle, the pale green of young corn or its ripe gold, the flower and seed coming on the hay fields. Or the brown of the spring ploughing, whitened here and there as the lime spreaders go roaring over it in low gear.

The outlook is very wide. From Galtee you look across to the shimmer of the Shannon, in the west are the Kerry mountains, in the east the Blackstairs, and to the south the undulating uplands of south Cork, with the sea beyond them. And set around the main ranges are smaller but attractive hills or groups of hills, the Ballyhoura, Slieve Reagh, Nagles mountains and the isolated Croughann Hill and Slievenamon.

The Galtees (40) trend east to west, a slim and slender range of high and grassy tops, rising to 3018 feet. Their character is essentially one of soft greens and changing clouds, which shadow their flanks or rise from the velvety ridgewalk of their crest. On the steeper, Tipperary, side the streams finger down the slopes like the strings of a harp, the silver music of these feminine mountains.

The Knockmealdowns (Knockmealdown, 2608 feet, variously translated as the bare brown mountain or as *Cnoc maoildomhnaigh*, Maoldomhnach's Hill) are different again. They are elongated east–west, but are a compact group of hills rather than a range. They are dark with heather, and cut by the deep gash of the V-road pass. From all angles they stand out a most symmetrical group, Knockmealdown itself a graceful cone with the subsidiary heights grouped about it. In detail they are humpy and fail to live up to the promise of the distant view; in reality a group of uplands commanding an outlook over all the plains around and with the church of the Cistercian abbey of Mount Melleray flashing white upon their flank. Yet the Knockmealdowns, if not exciting to the climber, have the virtue of never looking tame.

The Comeragh mountains (*cumarach*, abounding in hollows and river confluences) are different from both Galtee and Knockmealdown. Their trend is north to south, the northern portion being Comeragh, strictly speaking, and the lower, southern end, the Monavullagh mountains, less rocky and descending toward the sea.

The Comeraghs form a plateau, tilted toward the west, and ending in sheer cliff and corrie on their eastern margin. The summit is broad, often a waste of black peat hag, eroded to the underlying pink rock debris here and there, and in places impenetrable in wet weather.

These hills have about them a strange quality of light, of a

39 Ridge and corrie lake on the mountain line from Carrauntual to Coomakista and Waterville, Co. Kerry

40 The Galtee mountains from the south

THE COMERAGH MOUNTAINS

delicate colouring, the forestry plantations (which cling like a fur collar around all these mountain groups) leading to grassy slopes diversified with heather and gorse, the clouds often clustered about the crest which are hackly with torrs of pink conglomerate. Two things give character to the Comeraghs, their rocky corries and the nearness of the sea, so that the climber coming up on to their heights from the west sees of a sudden far below him the gleaming southern coast of Ireland and the pale bright blue of the sea.

The range is cut by two passes, each with an old track through it, the Gap in the north and the Dog's Pass in the south. North of the Gap is the fine height of Knockanaffrin (2478 feet, the peak of the Mass), a fine heathery walk from the west, which ends in a torr-broken ridge and a sudden fall to the eastern plain below. Looking up from that plain the mountain shapes itself into a most dramatic cone. And in spring all that level country is gold with gorse, great hedges of it which edge the long straight roads and tangled patches which cover the waste ground and climb the hillsides.

South from the Gap the mountain-top widens to the haggy plateau, and rises to its highest point, Knockaunapeebra (2597 feet, the little hill of the piper). On either side are corries, cut in the red rock, with green turf between the crags, and still water cradled beneath them. Small streams cataract down, and I have seen the wind, blowing hard against the rock, catch them and send their waterfalls spraying skyward. The finest corrie of the group is in the series on the east, Coumshingaun (*cúm seangán*, glen or corrie of the ants), a corrie like a text-book figure, with great rocky walls rising sheer from the water nearly a 1000 feet. The red is broken by the green of the grass that grows thick on the cliffs between the rocks, with tufts of heather with it. There is an elongated lakelet dammed in by a series of moraines below (gravel bars deposited from a glacier foot), which build a rumpled moundy mass spotted with enormous ice-carried boulders of conglomerate and under which caves and rock shelters abound. This alpine-looking lake and its cliffs (by following the lip of which one can gain the plateau top) lie within less than an hour's walk from the main road from Carrick-on-Suir to Dungarvan, and seem symbolic of the nature of this group of Irish hills, the mountain encircled and enveloped by the plain, the wildness of the hills surrounded by the civilisation of the lowland.

Lowland and mountain, the two extremes. I visited Coumshingaun on a morning that began with cloud and frost, gave place to sun and most extensive views, and then, as I stood looking at the two torr-hackled ridges which form the jaws of the corrie and at the lake itself, a strange metallic indigo-blue in colour, rain storms swept down upon the Comeragh heights and then into the corrie itself in a steady downpour; the thunder came in sudden bursts, roaring and echoing round the confining crags. I took shelter, like the hill sheep who looked wet and miserable peering out from the caves, under one of the great boulders on the moraine below the lake. From there I could look not only to the mist on the heights and the rain falling in a steady stream, but below to the coast, and through the thin curtain of the rain to the sun shining brightly on the coastal plain and on the sea, which lay still and quiet, a glittering blue. It struck me then as a thing symbolical, the conflict and the storm upon the heights, which those who would ascend will always need to face, whilst the dwellers on the plain, ambitionless, bask in the ease of sunshine and warmth, without the fierce excitements of the peaks of life.

These broken rocks are naturally good hiding-places, and, north a little from Coumshingaun, is the cave of Crotty, another famous Irish highwayman. The Comeraghs, then, seem to have carried natural woodland which gave additional protection to William Crotty and his men. William was hanged in 1742; his widow was also the object of pursuit and, tracked into the hills, killed herself by springing off Crotty's Rock above the cave.

Southward, the Dog's Pass, *bearna an madrara*, and perhaps more correctly the Wolf's Pass, has at its summit some standing stones, and attached to it a legend of St. Declan. All this country is associated with St. Declan, another pre-Patrician Irish saint, whose main church was on the coast at Ardmore. Here are extensive ruins and a fine round tower, and the saint still greatly honoured at the annual pattern on his day, July 24th. The story about the pass tells of a pagan chief called Dercan who tried to insult his guest by feeding him dog's meat disguised as mutton. Declan detected this, restoring the dog to life and sent it flying through the mountain gap!

THE GALTEE MOUNTAINS

It is a country of contrasts, the great cushions of heather around the rocks below Coumshingaun and not far off the green fields and woods of the lowland. Sometimes the one seems to mingle with the other, as on the hillsides round the Bay Lough, high in the gap of the V-road over Knockmealdown, where the rhododendrons grow in thickets and cover the mountain-side with pink blossom. The woods which run up the valley from Lismore toward the hills have blue wild hyacinths and blue wood anemones, giving place eventually to moorland and the gorse.

I saw the contrast best, following that same May storm of snow that blocked me on the Slieve Bloom track, when the Galtees were white and one looked up to them from a thicket of scarlet rhododendron and yellow gorse, growing on the bank of a mountainy-looking stream flowing fast over red pebbles.

The Galtee mountains (*Sliabh na gcoillteadh*, mountain of the woods) have justly been claimed as Ireland's finest inland mountains (40). They rise in a slender line north of the Mitchelstown–Caher road, with gentler slopes on their southern flank than on the north, where they fall steeply to the Glen of Aherlow, a down-faulted strip of Carboniferous rock. They are grassy, good pasture, and with a certain delicate grace, a single line of heights reaching up to the clouds of the summer's sky, or, dusted with snow in winter, contrasting with the green of the lowland around them.

Galtymore, 3018 feet, is easily climbed by its long shoulder reaching down toward the south, a walk up over short heather and grass to the little tableland of the summit with its fantastically shaped outcrops of conglomerate rock. The wind drives fiercely over that high and narrow crest: from it one looks to all the neighbouring hills, Comeragh and Knockmealdown, the Slieve Felims, the Kerry heights. Immediately below is the Glen of Aherlow and across it the parallel and lower ridge of the hill of the pig, Slievenamuck, 1216 feet. Down to that valley, Galtymore descends in a precipitous but grassy slope, at whose foot is the little corrie lake of Lough Curra. On either hand the Galtee ridge is an inviting ridgewalk, over short turf or heather, with here and there weathered peat hag stretches. West, one may continue on to Lyracappul (2712 feet) and the isolated Temple Hill which marks the western termination of the range;

eastward, walk on to Greenane (2630 feet), past a massive upstanding outcrop of conglomerate called, not unsuitably from its appearance, O'Loughnan's Castle. Under Greenane is another and larger corrie lake, backed by some attractive crags, Lough Muskry, and one can walk up to the hills from Aherlow, past this lake, first through the forestry plantations and then over the moorland. As you leave the woods there are a few older pines which mark the end of the woodland and offset the outlook back to the valley and its checkerboard of fields.

These rocks about the Galtee lakes are interesting from the botanical angle: Lough Muskry is the most inland station in Ireland for *Saxifraga spathularis*, and Lough Curra is one of the two Irish localities for *Arabis petraea* (northern rockcress). They are found here with others of the Irish alpine plants.

The rocks of the hills, and the old woodland of their flanks, provided cover for men in hiding. This part of Tipperary has been associated with Irish resistance right up to the present day. The Glen of Aherlow was also, in the past, one of the important communication lines of the country from east to west, and accordingly ground much fought over. It is a pleasant valley to traverse, from the shell of the Franciscan friary of Moor "abbey" at its western end. Moor "abbey" itself, after the Reformation, often formed a storm centre and was used as a fortress: even as late as the final conflict for Irish freedom after the First World War, the British attempted to blow it up because of the cover it provided, an attempt which fortunately failed.

Aherlow is peaceful enough today, with the carts coming into the creameries and the goats, chained in couples, grazing its roadsides. The streams descend very straight in little trenched courses from the Galtee heights, and, seeing them glittering after rain, the late T. J. Westropp suddenly realised that these were the harps of the legendary harper Cliu: that the streams of the northern flank of the west end of the hills do form two shimmering silver harps upon the green mountain flank.

So steep are the hillsides on the north that they do not seem to have encouraged the people to go up to booleys, as they did on the southern slopes. In 1940 an old man of eighty in the village of Kilbeheny still remembered the booleying and could point out some of the ruined huts. Each family had twenty to forty cattle on the hill and the grazing was free. The custom came to an end when the landlord put a rent of £3 a head on each beast, which effectively stopped the use of the hill grazing by making the cost too high to be profitable. Sometimes the old and sometimes the young people went to the booley huts, according to the amount of work that was required to be done on the farms below. They stayed up there, only coming down to go to Mass or bring the butter for sale, the whole summer and used to raise crops of potatoes on the hillsides near their huts.

Back on the other side of the ridge, west of Galbally and Moor Abbey, is the low ridge of Duntryleague (*Dun Trí Liag*, fort of the three pillar stones), with a fine Megalithic cromlech on its top and the ruin of a stone fort. Still going west there is the isolated hill of Slieve Reagh (*Sliabh riabhach*, the brindled mountain), craggy at its east end but sloping more gently to the west. At this west end is the complex of ring forts, and tumuli and old fields of Cush, recently excavated and dating from the late Bronze Age. It lies just where the modern fields give place to the moorland of the mountain-side, and is the oldest dated site of ring forts and souterrains in Ireland.

Whilst the Galtees are one of the most attractive hill groups in Ireland to climb, these lesser heights like Slieve Reagh equally repay investigation. I came up on to the summit of Slieve Reagh (1531 feet) one morning after early mist and rain, the long grass of the fields below drenched with dew. It was August, moist, damp, sunless. The heather was just into flower, tall ling in magnificent little bushes along the craggy northern edge of the little hill, and with blaeberries intertwined in it, with very large, fully ripe fruit. I began to pick them, watched by a stoat which ran round me inquisitively, and discovering, too, a nest of wild bees. As I picked the sun came through. The effect was almost magical. The damp air gave an intense colouring and clarity, close at hand were the red and grey rocks with the bright heather round them, below the green fields and hedges and woods, with the yellow squares of corn. And round were all the mountain ranges clear and distinct, with the mist rising to form cumulus over the green peaks of the Galtees, and northward the glint of the Shannon.

There is the same kind of view from the old Celtic church site of Ardpatrick, west of Kilfinnane, with the shell of an old **church** and the stump of a round tower. Ardpatrick is on the flank of the Ballyhoura mountains, which reach 1702 feet in Seefin Mountain. Here again is heather and rock, and one of the best places for picking blaeberries in the district. The Seefin slopes are in places almost blue with their fruit in August. And there is the outlook to the Galtees and the Tipperary and Limerick fields.

Very many of these hills, like Duntryleague, have cairns on their tops. There is a ruined one upon Seefin in the Ballyhoura mountains and tradition has claimed it for the burial-place of Oisin, Finn's son, the legendary poet—who must be buried on a considerable number of Irish and Scottish hills! The name Ballyhoura recalls another mythical hero, Feabhrat, of which there is an account in the Book of Leinster. The mountains are named from *Bealach Fheabhrat*, Feabhrat's Pass, which lies between them and Buttevat.

Southward are the Nagles mountains, which reach 1406 feet in Knocknaskagh. Their heights too are crowned with big cairns, but perhaps the most striking of the series is the much-ruined great cairn upon the little hill at Corrin just outside Fermoy, which rises steeply up from the main Cork–Fermoy road. Corrin Hill is only 727 feet, but is isolated and a very commanding height indeed. There is the trace of a hilltop fort here too, and rising from these ancient ruins a magnificent cross erected to mark the Holy Year of 1933. Meantime on the flank there is a little holy well, still visited occasionally. I tried to extract information about it from a woman I met on the road below, with little success except for the reiterated statement: "There is a cure in it." These Irish holy wells do, in point of fact, seem to continue to be associated with a few cures of physical ailments, though it is impossible to make any definite statement about them, as one can of those at Lourdes, because they have never been properly investigated and checked. There is a holy well just north of Slieve Reagh which attracts a big crowd at the annual pattern in August. It is near Martinstown, and is a powerful spring in a low-lying meadow; its patron is St. Molua. A concrete setting, statue of St. Molua, and a wall round, were put up by the local branch of Muintir na Tire in 1950 in honour of the Holy Year of that date and of the Assumption of Our Lady.

Human associations, then, are never far away, from the prehistoric cairns of the hilltops onward, in this country of the southern Irish mountains. The mountains spring up from the plain and the plain is rich not only in its soil and its grazing, but in its history.

Yet the mountains themselves are lonely. There is a small mountainy track of a road which scrambles up the Ballyhoura mountains, but otherwise the only important mountain road of the district is the V through the central pass of the Knockmealdowns from Clogheen to Lismore. On the low ground in that area, incidentally, there are still many thatched houses, some gable, some hipped roofed and magnificent examples of the art. The V road leaves the valleys and climbs through forestry plantations out on to the moors, with the plain of Tipperary spread like a checked tablecloth below it. On the southern side the road descends more gently, past Melleray where the Cistercians have wrought their fields from the moors and shown just what can be made of high-level mountain-side.

The V road is perhaps the best known of the Irish mountain roads. Yet it is only one of a series incredibly rich for so small a country with such a small area of high land. Not only the high-level roads of the Wicklows should be better known, but also those in West Cork and Kerry which take the motorist into the best of the hill country and right over the heights themselves.

CHAPTER IX

West Cork and Kerry

As you travel west into Kerry the land grows poorer and the red sandstones appear in little outcrops beside the road, swelling farther on into hills and mountains. In the east of Co. Cork the colouring is bright but without the depth and brilliance of the west: as you journey into Kerry the landscape changes, becoming progressively more vivid in colour and wilder in aspect.

It might be that you would come into Kerry by the main road from Cork to Killarney, where the hills begin just beyond Macroom with the red sandstone bearing a rock garden of heather and dwarf gorse. Or better, by the coast, where the headlands run out into a sea that becomes a deeper blue toward the west, or so it seems, and a country of small islands, long inlets, rough hill country. Here is the little port of Baltimore that gave its name to the more famous city across the Atlantic, and into it come the boats that will take you out to Sherkin Island and Cape Clear—rocky cliffs with the sea seething at their foot, and Sherkin itself a riot of wild flowers, fertile, with the substantial ruin of a Franciscan friary. Beyond, across the intricate shallows and islands of Roaring Water Bay, where the sea shades into delicate blues over the estuaries, is the village of Ballydehob, and above it Mount Gabriel rising to 1339 feet and with a small road snaking over its shoulder, putting the motorist within a brief walk of its crest.

Upon the rocky ridge that forms the broad back of Mount Gabriel one can make a beginning in the exploring of West Cork. Here the heather grows in luxuriant tussocks, often with occasional clumps of the white ling and bell varieties, on the rocks, but there is bog on the very top with rough grass orange tipped. The moist air carries the scent of bog myrtle and the heather flowers. Below, the little fields run far up the hillside

41 The lake and forest park of Gougane Barra, Co. Cork

42 The Healy Pass, on the Cork/Kerry border

in every valley, and lead down to the sea, an old castle showing like a broken tooth here and there along the lowlands. The sea fingers far inland in deep and narrow arms, *rias*—drowned valleys. From Mount Gabriel you look west across the whole succession of these inlets and peninsulas, Dunmanus Bay, Bantry Bay, and then to Hungry Hill above Castletownberehaven. Beyond lies Kerry and the inlet of the Kenmare River, and farther yet, out of sight, the last *ria* of the series, Dingle Bay. Inland, the Kerry mountains and those of West Cork rise in massive ridges, the Reeks of Killarney, the solid block of uplands at the back of Bantry, the outlying heights of Shehy, a commanding ridge standing in isolation on the eastern edge of the West Cork hills.

Geographically the county boundary between Cork and Kerry means very little. It runs down the backbone of the Beara peninsula, between Bantry Bay and the Kenmare River, but there is no change in the essential nature of the country, for that has already become apparent farther east.

Of the great mass of mountain country, mostly carved from red sandstone, which builds all the hill country of this part of Ireland, only a few of the hills are really exciting in themselves. The pattern of the heights is rather of a monotonous repetition of rock and boggy moorland in rounded massive haunches, with a certain majesty like the hind quarters of an elephant, but seemingly hardly worth the individual climbing of each. In Connemara each mountain has its own special character and invites ascent; in Kerry, one should select the outstanding mountains of the district, and then add to them what is indeed the particular flavour of this country, the exploration of the corrie lakes and of the coast and its cliffs and islands. All this district was heavily glaciated and the heights were smoothed and rounded by the ice, but along the rims of the uplands the glaciers plucked and pulled at the rocks and tore the craggy faces and hollowed out the tarns which lie below them. Only a few ridges rose above the ice, the Reeks, Mount Brandon and some others, which now show frost-riven splintered crests in contrast to the lower rounded hills. There was an ice-free area around the head of Dingle Bay too, and it seems that this was one of the areas in which the pre-glacial flora was able to weather the cold and survive.

It is a country of small farms and small fields, often worked by the spade. It is a country where Irish history creeps far up the mountain-side, a country where the mountaineer is never alone with his mountains but always tripping up on history, discovering little bits of the Irish past for himself and leaning over stone walls talking to men whose accents are the soft, Welsh-sounding ones of Kerry, and who lean upon spades or scythes. It is a countryside easier to get to know than that of the broad fields of the east: it is much easier to get into conversation with a farmer with a scythe than one driving a combine harvester.

It was a Kerryman mowing hay with the scythe that I stopped to ask the whereabouts of a carved stone, and to discuss the season. "Yes," said he, "we're backward here anyway, but this year we're more backward than usual." He indicated the monuments I was looking for. "There're two over there, by the cow," he said, pointing to what looked like a ruined Megalithic cairn, "but there're others above, below the new house, on the line of the old road, Daniel O'Connell's road we call it."

It seemed to me that here at Loher, below the pass of Coomakista, I touched on the essential blend of Kerry and West Cork. Here, near us, was a stone fort, above the little monastery of the Celtic church I was seeking, out to sea the dramatic rock of the Skellig with its sixth-century hermitage still intact, higher on the hills were copper mines that seem to have been worked from Bronze Age times. I went up to the Celtic site of Loher, a small monastic enclosure with the ruin of a beehive-vaulted oratory and some beehive cells, outside the little church was a slender pillar stone with a Latin cross on it, and the Alpha Omega. I felt that the Celtic monk leaving off tying a sheaf might say the same thing as the modern farmer—they were backward here in the west but not so backward as not to know some Greek: and earlier still, the Bronze Age miner on Coad Mountain might repeat the same expression—they might be far back in the hills, but not so far back as to fail to drive a bargain with the traders bringing tin from Spain and Cornwall.

To some extent the higher you go the older are the ruins you come upon, the cairns, the Celtic stone forts and hermitages; down by the sea it is more recent history, the castle of O'Sullivan Beare, the Franciscan friary of Sherkin Island, and almost in our own times, the tracks of that great Irishman, Daniel O'Connell, and his home at Derrynane close to the Coomakista Pass.

There is a moistness in the air in this country, a warm steaminess that not only originates the exotic pockets of Glengarriff and Parknasilla, but seems to temper the very sunlight and gives a softness peculiar to the colouring of this part of Ireland. If Connemara is crystalline in its brilliance, if the sea there is sapphire, here in Kerry the colouring is opalescent and the sea is lapis. In winter the snow may flash white from the heights for a short while, but in summer the sea is gentian blue, the rocks purple and pink intersected with green bog grass and moss and bracken, with yellow tussocks of dwarf gorse and the bright cushions of bell heather, the wild thyme spreading little mats of flower along the roadsides and the lanes overhung with almost incredibly tall fuchsia bushes.

And it was something of this that I saw, as it were in a sudden and unexpected summary, a few hours before I had gone down the hill to talk to the man at Loher. I had driven west from Cork and come over the mountains from Ballyvourney to Kenmare on a morning that in Cork had promised sun and shower, but in the West Cork mountains had degenerated into a drenching hill mist with only a few yards visibility. At Kenmare I came clear of the mist and saw a blink of sunshine and patches of light on the distant hills, but at Sneem it was worse again, with a bank of dull mist lying on the sea and the mountains wrapped in cloud and darkness.

In these conditions I turned the car up a muddy trail to Kilcrohane above West Cove on the north shore of the Kenmare River, slithering under dripping fuchsias to a halt below the two ruined churches in the old graveyard, with St. Crohaun's holy well (still visited on the annual pattern on July 30th) alongside. Crohaun, said to have been a contemporary of St. Patrick, blessed another well on Windy Gap Pass, on the ridge between Kilcrohane and the Waterville hollow, and on the same mountain-side he had a cave for hermitage. The original pilgrimage in his honour visited all three sites; now it only goes to the well at the graveyard.

The sea then lay steely grey, hidden for the most part in mist, and above me the same mist moved in snaking wreaths upon the heights. There were gleams of sunshine, the long grass was drenched with dew. The small fields edged up from the levels by the shore, far up the valley hollows, to the great stone fort of Staigue east of Kilcrohane, and above Kilcrohane itself, stone walls, small houses, little Kerry cows. I asked a man taking his cattle out to pasture for St. Crohaun's Cave. We climbed on to a small rock for him to point it out. "Keep up the stream," he told me, "and where you see the white stones, there is a ruin beside the stream and the cave is close beside it, low down." He added a delicious touch about crossing "a new bit of an old road" and warned me, as everybody in Ireland always seems impelled to do, about getting lost in the "fog".

So I climbed the slopes of Coad Mountain (*comhfod*, a grave or bed) beside a tumbling mountain stream, and came to the "white stones", a vein of quartzite associated with the copper ore that once was mined here. St. Crohaun took possession of one of the old quarry holes of the prehistoric workings for his hermitage. The white rock is enamelled with blue copper "bloom", for these copper ores weather in bright colours on the surface of the rocks in which they occur, turning the old workings of Allihies into something like the stories of Aladdin's Cave, with their streaks and patches of green and peacock blue.

I sat on the hillside beside the saint's cave and the ruined buildings and spoil heaps of more recent mining operations. I had climbed up in the mist, now the sun gained on it and the full clearing came with sudden brilliance. I found myself sitting in warm sun in the shelter of a rock, looking down upon the Kenmare River and the whole line of the mountains of the Beara peninsula on its farther side. The steel dullness of the sea gave place to a rich gentian blue, and the amorphous mist rose off the Beara hills and shaped itself into shining banks of white cumulus, whilst the mountains themselves appeared in all their sun-dappled shapeliness. And below was the green checker pattern of fields reaching up to the rough hill pastures.

I knew the Beara hills well enough to appreciate the sudden clearing, the higher Caha range giving place to the lower Slieve Miskish behind Castletownberehaven. I could identify the inlet of Kilmakilloge and look beyond Kilcatherine Point to the rocky snout of the Cod's Head and at the western end to the high cliffs of Dursey Island, the narrow sound that separates it from the

43 The hills of the Beara peninsula with Glanbeg lough and (extreme right) Hungry Hill

44 Mangerton, Killarney in winter with the head of the Horses' Glen and the Devil's Punch Bowl

45 Mangerton in summer with the distant view to the Lower Lake at Killarney

peninsula being concealed so that it looked like a part of the mainland.

The Caha mountains (*ceatha*, a shower) have, amongst their massive uplands and their hidden corrie lakes, two outstanding heights, the highest point, Hungry Hill (2251 feet), and the dramatic cone of the Sugar Loaf (1887 feet), which forms the completion of the Glengarriff picture of still water and shapely rock framed in pines. For the rest the Beara hills are of the usual blend of red sandstone rock alternating with bog, as monotonous to walk as it is attractive to look at, from the distance and across the bright sea.

The rightful name of Hungry Hill (43) is Knockdayd, or Cnoc Daod, and the late T. J. Westropp thought it might also be the Sliabh Diadche up which, according to the Book of Lismore, St. Brendan climbed to plan his voyage and from which he looked down upon "the mighty intolerable ocean on every side". The English Hungry Hill is an intriguing title, it goes back beyond 1655, but there is no explanatory tradition of the name.

However named, Knockdayd would attract the climber, its rocky bulk reared in a long ridge from the calm sea of the inlet of Adrigole Harbour on Bantry Bay. At the head of the inlet the road divides, one branch leading round the snout of Hungry Hill for Castletownberehaven, the other going over the Healy Pass in a gradual but serpentine series of bends, one of the great mountain roads of this part of Ireland. Meantime, a dusty track leads up from Adrigole pier into the cluster of small farms cradled in the hollow formed by the two eastern spurs of the mountain.

I came to Adrigole on an April day, when the sun was bright but the wind was keen, yet all the distance was hidden in a haze, so that the blue of the sky sloped down to a brown curtain blanketing the horizon. That is often the case; fine weather and haze; storms and clear views. The woods were fresh in new leaf, with bright patches of primroses and bluebells, and at Adrigole the yellow gorse fringed the small fields. Holly showed its glossy leaves in the hedges, a native tree very common in Kerry and West Cork (I suppose its abundance is due to the fact the cattle cannot eat it); fuchsia bushes mingled with it. As I walked up the southern spur of Hungry Hill I looked back to the settlement in the glen, fields and whitewashed houses, the river, the sea beyond, the valley floor moulded into ridges by the passage of the ice, so that it looked like a crumpled quilt. The glaciation is more marked above, the mountain rising into two great sandstone walls, with the shelf between them hollowed to cradle two glittering corrie lochans. The two ends of this great line of rock are less precipitous; the southern one indeed appears formidable from the distance but is in reality a straightforward ascent.

The southern spur itself bears turf cuttings on its back, and in it the roots of old firs are exposed. One looks down to Bantry Bay and Bere Island, plumes of smoke rising from muir burnings. I thought of Carew's account of 1602, of the great harbour of Berehaven, the sheltered water between the island and the land, "Berehaven . . . of capacitie sufficient to contain all the ships of Europe."

From the other side of the ridge I could now look down on the smaller of the two corrie lakes: Coomarkane, still, dark water, edged with yellowish grass and ringed with the pink and violet sandstone of the mountain; a spur of rock separates it from its northern companion, Coomadavallig. It is typical West Cork and Kerry mountain, this, on Hungry Hill's shoulder, a multitude of rocky faces, smooth on one side, polished by the ice, and plucked into a crag face on the other. The gullies between frame the view to the sea. Tufts of heather and dwarf gorse grow on the rocks and make a brilliant show of flower in late summer; here too is the pale pink of St. Patrick's cabbage. It is country amusing to scramble about on, but with troublesome elements in that the sheer walls of the sandstone are devoid of holds and not easy to spot from above, so that the unwary may find himself "pounded" on the steeper descents. There have been accidents on these hills, particularly in the Killarney area, and their rocks should be treated with respect.

The southern end of Hungry Hill is, however, a pleasant scramble over the rocks, leading up to the white quartzite vein which marks the summit at this end, and whose superior hardness has probably determined the shape of the top here. After the enjoyment of rock and the prospect of sea and coast below, the summit of Hungry Hill comes as anticlimax. This so rocky mountain is, on its top, a broad and level plateau of boggy grass on which the sheep graze. Walking from one to the other of the cairns on it you see nothing of the crags that circle it unless you go to the edge and look down to the blue eye of Coomadavallig.

The northern end descends in a series of giant steps of sandstone to the col above this second corrie lake, and to a great waste of moor and sandstone which provides a high-level walk to the head of the Healy Pass (42). Only then, from the lake itself, does one realise the quality of the Knockdayd cliffs, as they rise from the still water, red and violet crag faces, with gullies and pinnacles. The lochan itself spills over the ice-moulded lip of its basin and down the heights to Adrigole in a silver ribbon of a waterfall.

Other spurs lead back down to the valley and provide a good route back to Adrigole. Moor gives place to short turf, and there are the shells of booley huts which once allowed the cattle to make use of this sweet bite of mountain grass.

In clear weather Hungry Hill is one of the great view-points of these hills, an outlook to sea and peninsula and the springing rock of Skellig of St. Michael out to sea.

It was in equally hazy weather, the land shimmering with heat, that I explored beyond Hungry Hill to the very tip of the Beara peninsula and Dursey Sound. Skellig that day was a spectral height appearing above the brown haze on the sea. Yet despite the heat, the sea, calm in the sheltered *rias*, was running in a heavy swell on the headlands, with white breakers sending spray smoking inland.

In June a great change had come on the country since my April climb on Hungry Hill. The trees were in full leaf and the rhododendrons in flower, the water lilies out on the little lakes and the first bell heather in flower, the rocks were tufted with thrift and the St. Patrick's cabbage formed a froth of pink on the grey rock faces by the roadside. The road, passing the southern spur of Hungry Hill, comes into Castletownberehaven and an unexpected oasis green, and wooded. O'Sullivan Beare's fortress here was the last of the strongpoints along the coast to yield after Kinsale. Beyond the town the trees end, and ahead are the humpy Slieve Miskish mountains, devoid of striking features; interest is centred on the coast, the sheer cliffs and the offshore rocks and stacks. Dursey Island itself continues the same sort of country seaward and is separated from the mainland only by a narrow and cliff-bound sound. Two other narrow clefts, through which the sea has not yet eaten its way, lie to the east and carry the road back and forth across the narrow tip of the peninsula, dramatic little passes with steep hillsides and the sea sparkling below at either end.

Through one such pass one can come down to Allihies, the line of cliff broken by the broad sandy beach of Ballydonegan. Beyond, Allihies village itself straggles up the hillside to the old copper mines, the mountain honeycombed with shafts and trenches, ruined mine buildings desolate upon the heights. Half Allihies itself seems in ruin, deserted miners' houses—it almost appears as if it had been bombed: the new Catholic church is a startling white, with its bell outside slung from a pylon of rusted iron whose origin one suspects was with the mines.

Another, higher pass, takes one over the shoulder of the Slieve Miskish and back to Castletown. Descending, Berehaven is spread before one, with Hungry Hill rising massively, and the town itself, with its encircling trees and small blue lakes, set in the lowland.

Just as Hungry Hill commands this western end of the Beara peninsula, so does the Sugar Loaf (*Slieve na Goill*, the mountain of mist) the eastern end above Glengarriff. Its conical symmetry suggests a kind of Irish Matterhorn, a savage struggle with bare rock and overhanging crags; in reality, the appearance is deceptive and the hill tails out into a long ridge up whose flank one may scramble easily over the grass to the summit in less than an hour from the little road below.

Slieve na Goill's great attraction is the outlook from it; the whole of Bantry Bay, and line upon line of mountains, the Kerry hills on the one hand and those of West Cork on the other. There are the rounded Paps of Dana, the tooth of Shehy, the rocks of the Reeks, and eastward the undulating fields of the lower and more fertile districts. Below the mountain lie steep-walled glens, with a corrie lake green in its reflection of the circling hillside. The small fields creep up these valleys from the Glengarriff–Kenmare road, in summer a patchwork of different coloured crops and separated one from the other by thick leafy hedges, so that each plot appears from above circled with a frilled ruff of green. Meantime the small fields on the south side of the Sugar Loaf still come fairly high, but not so high as formerly, and there is a whole deserted hamlet just below its final rise to the ridge.

So I looked down upon Castletownbere and Hungry Hill, upon the sea and the little blue lakes, as I came from Allihies, and I remembered in the blueness of these lakes a certain mountain lake in South Uist in the Hebrides and Neil Munro's description of it, "so blue that no other water in the Long Island can compare with it for loveliness", and now, as I came down Slieve na Goill to the ruined houses, I recalled another phrase from the same book. "There has been no dance in Corodale for two generations. Still the crash of seas, and Corodale Loch in sunshine blue as an angel's eye: still the mountains, but never again the men."*

Everyone in Kerry and West Cork will find out their own favourite mountain and group of corrie lakes, or select some special strand and headland which particularly appeals to them. But the essential nature of the country is much the same as here on Hungry Hill and Slieve na Goill, the brilliance of the sea and mountain leading back into a more massive and less highly coloured inland mountain block. The roads which traverse this country are not to be despised; they cross the very heart of the hills, commanding the same sort of outlook as the summits themselves. Coomakista, rounding the peninsula which lies between the Kenmare River and Dingle Bay, climbs high and looks seaward out to Skellig; farther on, from Cahirciveen inland toward Killorglin, this same route runs in a terrace on the hillside above the sea, across which lie the Blasket Islands and Mount Brandon. Meantime, the Beara peninsula is crossed by the really alpine road of the Healy Pass and farther east, the main road from Glengarriff to Kenmare climbs high too, tunnelling through the summit rocks. Its continuation from Kenmare to Killarney climbs up to Windy Gap with all the famous lakes spread out far below it.

Across in the Dingle peninsula the Connor Pass climbs over the shoulder of Mount Brandon from Dingle to Stradbally. In the east, less well known, is the minor road up the tumbling Coomhola River from the head of Bantry Bay and right over the main ridge down to Kilgarven. More for walking than for driving is the grass-grown old track parallel to this road which

* *Children of Tempest.*

goes up by the Priestsleap over the flank of Coomhola Mountain. Under Shehy Mountain, above Inchigeela, is yet another mountainy track that takes one within a short distance of Shehy summit (1797 feet), from which one looks on the one hand to the mountains of the west and on the other to the fields of the east. South of Shehy another small road makes a fine route through the Cousane Gap. Again, another small road goes down the southern side of Bantry Bay and snakes over the ridge of hills that forms the spine of this peninsula which ends in the point called the Sheep's Head, and from which all the high mountains of Beara are seen in a kind of panoramic strip.

Most dramatic of all these roads is probably the Ballachbeama Gap (*bealach béime*, pass of the cut or blow). It is on a rough little road that leads north from Sneem over the hills to Killorglin. The valley is at first open, with massive mountains round it, small farms and turf cuttings in the bogs, the lake of Lough Brin. Quite suddenly, one rounds a bend and faces the pass, a narrow cut down through the mountain line that extends from the head of the Killarney lakes west to Mullaghanattin (*mullach an aitinn*, hill of the gorse) and beyond. It seems to be a cleft cut through the ridge, like so many, by a short-lived torrent of the waning phases of the glacial ice. It cut down through the hill in a sheer and narrow defile, whose floor and flank are littered with a waste of boulders, but it did not persist long enough to widen out the cleft, which is now a dry windgap. The rough little track has just room to slip through. The summit is 852 feet above the sea, and the crags rise immediately from there up to the 1505 feet of Knockavulloge and within a mile to the 2539 feet of Mullaghanattin itself. The road creeps out again from the rocks into spacious country north of the pass, level uplands of moor and farm, from which spring the highest mountains in Ireland, the great ridge of the Mac Gillycuddy's Reeks.

CHAPTER X

Mount Brandon and Carrauntual

IT is in Kerry that the highest ground in Ireland is to be found, in the Reeks rising to 3414 feet in Carrauntual, whilst the second highest group of Irish hills lies just across Dingle Bay, the 3127 feet of Mount Brandon. And whilst these two are a part of the typical Kerry and West Cork scene, they do, as it were, form two distinct enclaves within it and have their own special character. Mount Brandon's corries and crags are linked with the sea and the islands and with one of the richest districts in the country in early beehive buildings and in Ogam stones: the Reeks are intimately associated with the special and particular beauty of Killarney and its lakes.

I have come west to the Dingle peninsular, over the hills from Cork, past the symmetrical Paps of Dana, each with its massive summit cairn, and on through Glenflesk to Killarney, with the rocky hills standing in sharp relief against a blue-black stormy sky and the arch of a rainbow spanning the road ahead. And I have seen the sea running in thunderous surf on the rock-bound coast of Slea Head. It is a country of stormy seas, this westernmost edge of Ireland (the Blasket Islands "the next parish to America" as the saying is) and the Killarney mountains attract a very heavy rainfall. Yet perhaps nowhere in Ireland is the phrase "sun-drenched" more apt: whether you are on the red rocks of the Dingle peninsula, cushioned with heather and dwarf gorse, looking out to the islands rising in cliff and sward from a sea incredibly blue; or in the silence of the Killarney woods, walking amongst the trees from which the hills rise rockily, and with a stillness broken only by the twitter of the birds and the plash of streams.

It is also country of great geological interest. The hills are mostly sandstone, but with rocks of igneous origin in the Glenflesk-Mangerton district, which represent the volcanic activity that was associated with the Old Red Sandstone period in many areas. Yet it is the remains of the glacial period that are of the most interest in this country. They are exceptionally well preserved, and here one can see the fretted rocks of the ridges that rose above the ice, the typical ice-deepened glens like the famous Gap of Dunloe (48), ice-smoothed rocks, and corries formed by glaciers nourished in them into precipice walled tarns. On the lower ground the glacier foot is marked by moraines, banks of gravel and sand deposited from its melting edge, and these moraines often dam back lakes.

North from Killarney one crosses the lowland at the head of Dingle Bay and then heads westward down the Dingle peninsula under the high wall of the Slieve Mish mountains (perhaps *Sliabh Meissi*, mountain of phantoms). The Slieve Mish form the landward end of the mountain backbone of the peninsula, while Mount Brandon rises toward its western end.

High on Slieve Mish is the stone fort of Caherconree, actually a fortified spur whose cliffs provide part of the structure's defences, and set 2050 feet above the sea. The tradition is that it was the fort of a king of Munster called Curoi MacDaire, and it is one of the three forts named in the Triads:

> The three forts of Ireland: Dunseverick, Dun Cermna (Old Head of Kinsale), Caher Conree.

As you continue westward the mountain scenery becomes wilder. The hills are rounded to the east, rugged toward the west. They end eventually in the line of the Blasket Islands, whilst Mount Brandon rises above Dingle town itself, a great barrier across the peninsula trending south to north. It is poor country agriculturally, once apparently wooded but now nearly treeless, and with small fields and small farms and primitive methods of working them. The stone walls are often very thick: they are constructed of the stones collected off the fields they enclose, and there are often beehive-shaped piles of the same stones set upon the actual field, usually heaped on a boulder too big to move. On Slea Head slopes are steep, and you may see the harvest carried on a rough sled drawn by a pony.

Under Mount Brandon and from Ventry to Slea Head, which is the westernmost point, the hillsides are quite literally covered with the ruins of beehive houses. Stone is so abundant that to

46 The Pedlar's lake, Connor Pass, Co. Kerry

47 The Macgillycuddy Reeks, Co. Kerry

48 The Gap of Dunloe, Co. Kerry

build and roof in it is the obvious economic thing to do. Over on the north side of the peninsula, at Gallarus, is the finest specimen surviving of a beehive-vaulted, stone-built (in drystone, without mortar) Celtic oratory. It is intact; others in various stages of ruin or preservation are to be found on the hillsides round about and on the small Celtic hermitages that were established on the smaller Blasket Islands and on the Magheree Islands. Stone-built beehives are still in use and constructed by the people for use as toolsheds, hen houses and the like. The beehive villages of Mount Brandon side and Slea Head perhaps date from the early Christian period, like the oratories; they represent the same sort of farming economy that is still carried on by the people here. Associated with the Celtic church sites are a fine series of early Celtic cross pillars, and there is a fine Irish Romanesque church at Kilmalkedar.

Here, too, are many forts. The headlands lend themselves naturally to fortification. Perhaps the finest headland fort in Ireland is Dun Beg (the little fort) to the east of Slea Head. It is defended both by banks and fosses, and a stone wall. The actual westernmost tip of Ireland is a headland fort likewise, Dunmore (the big fort). On the north coast of the peninsula is Smerwick. It was here in 1580 at Dun an Oir (the fort of gold) that the garrison of Irish and Spanish troops were massacred by the English forces to whom they had surrendered.

It is country mostly Irish speaking, though with unexpected little pockets of English speakers, and it is still rich in tradition and story. And it is the coast where the finest and largest of the Irish curraghs are to be seen. These descendants of the skin-covered wicker boat, now made of tarred canvas, are to be found all along the west coast, from the small, squat ones of Tory in Donegal, down through the graceful little boats of Aran and Connemara, to these of Kerry (5). Normally rowed, they sometimes rig a small sail; they are light ("giddy" as the Kerryman told me), but fast and very seaworthy, able to live in much rougher water than a wooden boat. They can also be lifted ashore and up the cliffs into safety, a great virtue on these rocky coastlines.

Brendan was a Kerry man, born at Annagh near Tralee in 484, and these were some of the types of boats with which he was familiar on his sea journeys. But he also climbed the hills and

Mount Brandon is St. Brendan's Mountain, *Cnoc Brennain*. The very top has a good spring of fresh water, the only one actually on the long ridge, and here the saint had a stone-built cell and oratory, of which the ruins still stand. It remains one of the mountain pilgrimages of Ireland and lately efforts have been made to revive greater interest in it.

The quickest way up Mount Brandon is by the pilgrim track, "The Saint's Road" from Ballybrack up a gently sloping spur of the mountain. Yet to appreciate the hill, one of the loveliest of Irish mountains, the full traverse of the great ridge should be made. One can begin in the south by ascending one of the spurs there and then continue north, over the summit and on to the final cliffs above the sea. Before these are reached an old cross-country track leads down the lowland again near Ballinknockane. The western side of the mountain is grass and heather, and the cattle graze right up to the summits, but these slopes end with dramatic suddenness on the east, in precipice, boulder-strewn crag foot and crystal lake.

As one climbs up the view widens out at one's back, till all the peninsula and the Blasket Islands lie spread below, with the Reeks rising across the sea to the south. To come up from the spur that leads up to the rocky Brandon Peak, at a height of 2764 feet on the main ridge, is to see the outlook on the east side all of a sudden, Brandon Bay and its sandy beaches (5), the Seven Hogs or Magheree Islands, and far inland to the east and northward up the coast. All this bursts on the climber in the instant that he breasts the crest of the crag, and he sees below him, with equal suddenness, the rocks and cliffs and the dark corrie lakes of the mountain's crags.

The ridge itself undulates along, keeping above 2500 feet, pleasant sward to walk, and with the drama of the cliffs close at hand all the while. Here are pinnacles, here are mural crags, here boulder beds at their foot, their colours change with the varying light and shadow. Here then lie corrie lakes of inky blackness in the shadow, and here are others in the sun of vivid blue, or crystalline in their clearness, so that you look down through their pale greenish depths. Between them, linking one lake with another, are the white icing sugar strings of cascades.

And beyond, the colours of the sea, its blues varying with the increasing depths, the knife-edge ridge of the Great Blasket, the green Magherees, the yellow sands, the ragged line of the Reeks. In clear weather one may see the Connemara hills.

The Reeks above Killarney have something of the same character, ice-fretted crag and corrie lake, but I think, less spectacularly developed than on Brandon, and likewise, since they stand a little inland, and do not like Brandon span a narrow peninsula, they lack that mountain's special association with glittering sea and clustered islets.

This line of hills, trending east–west and rising to the west of the Killarney lakes, is properly called in full, the Mac Gillycuddy's Reeks (47). Mac Gillycuddy was the name of the local chief and means the son of the servant of St. Mo-chuta, *Mac Gilla Mo-chuta*. Mo-chuta is the Irish name of St. Carthage (died 637), the founder of the great Celtic monastery of Lismore, and like Brendan a Kerryman, born at Castlemaine. The word Reek is used in Ireland for a mountain ridge. Perhaps the basic idea is a rick shape, or the rig that the Scots apply to some uplands. Croagh Patrick in all the country round about it is always called The Reek.

The highest point of the ridge of the Reeks, Carrauntual, is *Corran tuathail*, the inverted reaping hook, as usually translated, though it has been suggested that the name means Toole's Cairne, *Carn tuathail*. It forms a rounded shoulder, partly crag-encircled, at the western end of the ridge. From it the narrow, steep-sided line of hills form an undulating ridge, easy to walk along with its short mossy turf, until, toward the gap of Dunloe, its character changes and in Knocknapeasta (hill of the *piast*, some species of water kelpie) ends in a hackle of rock, of knife-edge and crag that is reminiscent of the Cuillin of Skye. The traverse of this crest calls for rock-climbing but the route may be continued by the less agile or expert by descending somewhat down the hillside below the worst of the rocks.

The Reeks are part of the Killarney scene, and it is perhaps that way one should come to them, over the Windy Gap road from Kenmare, when the lakes lie sparkling below and the hills rise up steeply from them; or perhaps from Glenflesk, by the little track that skirts Lough Guitane and from which the whole line of the hills appears in an unexpected vista as the road mounts the slope out of the Glenflesk hollow, with, furthermore, a prospect of the Killarney lakes and their wooded islands.

Killarney stands to the rest of Ireland as the Trossachs stand to the Scottish Highlands, and it has indeed something, tempered by a much warmer climate, of the Trossach type of beauty. It is a blend of lake and hill, hill rising rockily from the water's edge, its lower slopes clothed in native wood, whilst from the heights not only are the mountains seen but the wide plain of the lowland country which extends to the hillfoot here and to the sea.

The whole may be conveniently observed from the top of Mangerton, which provides a bird's-eye view of all the Killarney country, and whose 2756 feet can be gained in under two hours from the road end above Muckcross. There is a kind of a track up to the corrie lake named the Devil's Punch Bowl, and the summit is some 500 feet above, over short moss and rush.

From Mangerton one sees the lakes, with their wooded islands, the woods along their shore, the mountains round one and the stately line of the Reeks. Across the shoulder of the hill itself one looks down the length of the Kenmare River and to the Beara peninsula. On the other hand to Dingle Bay and the peninsula's mountains; below to the flat land at the head of that inlet, and to Killarney itself with the cathedral spire reared above its houses. Rock and wood and lake, the cumulus of the sky reflected in the mirror-smooth Lough Leane, and Mangerton itself, the Kerry blend of boggy upland and rock-cut corrie.

Mangerton, it seems, rose clear from the ice but retained its broad-shouldered flat summit. Its glaciers, however, worked back into the face of the upland massif, and cut not only the small Devil's Punch Bowl, but the really dramatic gorge of the Horse's Glen (*Glenacappul*) to the east of it. Here crags descend to the narrow floor of the corrie, which cradles three lakes, set one above the other, as the ravine twists out from the mountain heart and down toward the lowland to the north.

Mangerton is *Mangartagh*, the mountain of hair-like grass, the hairy one. I thought it was an odd name until I climbed it. It is heather moor up to the Devil's Punch Bowl, and above the final rise looks singularly green. This green is a thick cover of moss, and growing in it are close-set clumps of short rushes. The mountain literally has a bristly, hairy appearance from these tufts of rush. Its summit is level boggy moor, now deeply cut by a bog burst, which has left a great gash and spread of raw peat near the top. I walked it dryshod when the whole hilltop was frozen hard, and the hag cuts edged with sheets of ice and icicles, but it would be unpleasant enough in wet weather. This is the hill, incidently, that recorded 141 inches of rain in 1903.

From Mangerton summit one can ridgewalk round the lip of the Horse's Glen to Stoompa and so down again to the lowland by Lough Guitane; but by descending in the opposite direction, by the stream from the Devil's Punch Bowl, one arrives on the line of the old Killarney–Kenmare road and in the Killarney woods. The moorland falls fairly steeply down to the valley of the old track, and as you descend over the rough trussocks the rocky cone of Torc Mountain (the boar's hill) on whose 1764 feet one looks down from Mangerton, begins to rise beneath one, with the woodland growing far up its rocks. The old track runs beneath it, through the woods, partly of new plantations of larch and pine and hemlock, partly of the native holly and oak, and brings one back to Muckcross, passing the Torc waterfall, where the stream descends to Muckcross Lake.

Under Torc the open valley narrows to a tree-clothed gorge, and one walks through a part of the old native woodland of Ireland. There is another relic of native forest up in the Lough Gill area near Ben Bulben, but this of Killarney is the best known and most studied. It must originally have clothed all the now rather bare hillsides—one cause of its destruction was iron smelting; there are the remains of old iron works near Lough Caragh, for instance, which was in operation till the mid-eighteenth century, by which time they had used up the available timber. The Killarney woodland is a luxuriant jungle, in which both trees and the rocks among which they grow are heavily coated with epiphytes—mosses, liverworts, ferns, ivy. It means that the timber is of little use commercially, this felt of vegetation, but it gives the hillside woods an exotic wildness.

The trees themselves include the arbutus, for this is the district where the Mediterranean flora is best developed, and the bogs round about are bright in their season with the large flowered butterwort (which climbs as high as 2250 feet up the hills). These arbutus trees of Killarney grow up to thirty feet in height, so sheltered are the glens, whilst in the Mediterranean area they only form bushes. With the arbutus are native oaks, holly, birch (a tree most beautiful at every season, crimson twigged in winter, then in pale leaf, in autumn brilliant gold) and yew. With these native trees are various introduced species which have established themselves in the congenial climate. Rhododendrons are everywhere to be seen, for example. The woodland climbs some 600 to 700 feet up the mountain-sides; higher the alpine flora is poorer than that of the north-west. The mountain ridges tend to be rather bare, rock and moss, rough grass and rush.

It is of course to Carrauntual and its ridges that one instinctively makes a way. Perhaps the ideal introduction to that peak is from Lough Acoose to the west of it. A rough road runs beside this upland lake, which is sited at a level of some 500 feet above the sea. From it a shoulder, diversified with craglets, brings one in the course of a short walk to the splendid corrie under Caher and Carrauntual. At the mouth of this high glen is the small Lough Eigher, set just back from it, at a higher level, the larger rock-circled Coomloughra Lough, whose head is named Lough Eagher. From its dark, wind-rippled waters the hillsides rise steeply, on the north to the grass and rocky outcrops of Skregmore (2790 feet), at the head in precipitous rock to Carrauntual itself. From Carrauntual a rock ridge leads to a sudden rise to Caher (3200 feet) and then more open slopes descend again to the southern side of the corrie. I saw it early in March, in bright sun, with the higher rocks etched with hard frozen snow, whilst a haze hid the detail of the outlook westward, to the fine mountain group between Cahirsiveen and Lough Caragh. This great rocky ridgeway, which is, I suppose, from the start at Lough Eighter and back to the same point a matter of between four and five miles, is claimed as the finest of all Irish ridgewalks. Its traverse involves some rock scrambling.

The "tourist" route up Carrauntual is via the so-called Devil's Ladder, a gully which leads up the flank of the main ridge of the Reeks from the north side and which equally provides an easy way up to make the traverse of the whole line of the tops toward the east.

There is a track up beside the west bank of the Gaddagh River to the foot of the Devil's Ladder. It is a pleasant route, this, with the whole line of the Reeks springing up from the lowland as you approach the starting-point, and all the lanes with great hedges of yellow gorse. I climbed this way once early in April after late snow. The gorse was in full flower, its gold contrasted against the scattered hollies of the rough lowland, moor and small fields and farms, littered with stones. The Gaddagh River flows in pools and rapids in a bouldery cut. It brings one eventually to the two corrie lakes in which it rises, set under the ridge of the Reeks, Lough Callee and Lough Gouragh. As one approaches, the western hillside above is broken into ragged rocks and screes called, not unsuitably, the Hag's Teeth. Carráuntual rises from Lough Gouragh in rock and littered scree, but the route lies between the two corrie lakes and up the gully, a simple enough scramble even if the early tourists did try and make out that the Devil's Ladder was a dangerous adventure! Not so pleasant, in fact, this April day, when the cleft was partly filled with rotten and melting snow-drifts into which one sank over the knee.

Once out at the top, a brief walk over the broad stony back of the main ridge brings one to Carrauntual summit. (The Ordnance maps, incidently, use the less elegant spelling of Carrauntoohil for this mountain, and there are other variants to be found as well.)

So in less than three hours from leaving the plain, with its gorse, and Killarney, with its gardens bright with spring flowers, I came out on an alpine Carrauntual top, where the Caher ridge carried heavy cornices of snow, the main ridge partly covered likewise, and with an icy wind keening over the height of Ireland.

On a clear day the outlook from this mountain is worthy of its position as the highest summit in the country. It commands all the ridges and sea inlets of Kerry and West Cork, and the low country round Killarney town and toward Tralee. Mountain ridge, sea, strand, moorland, and immediately below the beautiful lakes which lie in a cluster, like a necklace of beads, round the mountain crest. The tiny blue eye hidden in a wilderness of broken rock just below the summit itself, the Coumloughra group under the great ridgeway, Curraghmore to the south, and the Gaddagh River's two source lakes to the north. The line of the Slieve Mish continues along the Dingle peninsula to the crags of Mount Brandon, the blue sea of the bay ending against the white sands of Inch. Across the blue expanse of Lough Caragh, set in the lowland, rise the massive, corrie-cut group of hills west of that lake, rising to 2541 feet in Coomacarea.

And, blue-shadowed, dappled with snow, every ridge and cleft in its rocks picked out in white, the plunging line of the great ridge of the Reeks itself, leading east to the ragged spine of Knocknapeasta.

For the Holy Year of 1950 a wooden cross in a concrete setting was erected beside the summit cairn of Carrauntual. Across the inlet of Dingle Bay rises the ridge of Brandon with St. Brendan's hermitage upon its top, the second highest mountain group, and linking up the early Irish saints' love of the hilltops with the modern Irishman's setting up of crosses on the heights. Round the base of the Carrauntual cross are written two phrases, one in Irish and one in Latin:

> Do chum glóire De & onóra na h Eireann. (For the glory of God and honour of Ireland.)

and:

> Gloria in excelsis Deo et in terra pax hominibus bonae voluntatis. (Glory to God in the highest and on earth peace to men of good will.)

Index

Aasleagh, 32, 35
Achill, 32, 45
Aghla More, 62
Aherlow, Glen of, 23, 125, 126
Allihies, 136, 142
Altan Lough, 62
Antrim Hills
Arbutus, 18, 153
Ardara, 56
Ardpartick, 127
Arra mountains, 82

Ballaghbeama Gap, 144
Ballydonegan, 142
Ballyhoura mountains, 128
Ballykinvarga, 74
Ballyvaghan, 68
Barnesbeg Gap, 64
Barnesmore Gap, 55, 65
Beara Peninsula, 133, 136
Beehive houses, 146
Ben Baun, 36
Ben Brack, 36 41
Ben Breen, 37, 38
Ben Bulben, 47, 52, 67, 153
Bencollaghduff, 37
Ben Corr, 37
Ben Creggan, 35
Ben Cullagh, 36
Benevenagh,
Ben Gorm, 28, 32, 34, 35
Ben Gower, 37, 38
Ben Lettery, 38
Blackstairs mountains, 89, 100
Blue Stack mountains, 56
Booleys, 24, 34, 45, 110, 126
Brocken spectre, 102
Bronze Age cairns, 19, 112, 127
Burren, 67

Caha mountains, 136, 139
Caherconree, 20, 146
Cahercommaun, 73
Cappanawalla, 72
Carlingford, 116
Carrauntual, 15, 145, 151, 154
Carrick, 57
Ceanaille, 74
Celtic Church sites, 20, 41, 55, 57, 74, 76, 87, 92, 101, 116, 128, 134, 135, 149
Clachans, 24
Clareen, 87
Clew Bay, 44
Coad, 134, 136
Comeragh mountains, 119, 120
Connemara, 28
Connor Pass, 143
Coomadavallig, 140
Coomakista, 134, 143
Coomarkane, 140
Coomhola, 143
Coomloughra, 154
Corrin Hill, 128
Coumshingaun, 123, 124
Croagh Patrick, 20, 28, 32, 44, 77, 113, 151
Cuildrevne, 55
Curlew mountains, 81, 99
Curraghs, 149
Cush, 23, 127

Delphi, 31, 33
Derryclare, 36, 37
Derrynane, 135
Derryveagh mountains, 56, 63
Devil's Bit, 82, 87
Devil's Ladder, 154
Devil's Mother, 43

157

INDEX

Devil's Punch Bowl, 152
Diamond Hill, 41
Diamond Rocks, 114
Dingle Peninsula, 145
Dog's Pass, 123, 124
Donald's Hill
Donegal, 47
Doon Rock, 64, 76
Doughruagh, 32, 41
Drumlins, 44
Dublin Hills, 89
Dunfanaghy, 64
Dunlewy, 62
Dunloe Gap, 146
Duntryleague, 127
Dursey Island, 136, 141

Eagles, 45
Errigal, 15, 55, 56, 58, 62
Errisbeg, 32, 38

Fanad Head, 64
Field patterns, 23
Finn, the Fiana and the Finnian Tales, 46, 51, 76, 81, 115, 128
Flora of the hills, 18, 53, 58, 68, 126
Four Masters, 65

Galtee mountains, 119, 120, 125
Galtymore, 15, 125
Gartan, 63
Geology of the hills, 16, 104
Glaciation, 17, 36, 38, 63, 89, 133, 146
Glenade, 52
Glendalough, 90, 91, 92
Glen Car, 52, 53
Glencolumbkille, 57, 62
Glencree, 91
Glengarriff, 135, 139, 142
Glengesh, 62
Glen Imail, 97
Glen Inagh, 32, 36, 37, 42
Glenmacnass, 90

Glenmalure, 90, 91, 94
Glens of Antrim, 78
Gold, Irish, 90
Greenane, 126
Grianan of Ailech, 64

Healy Pass, 143
Hill of Allen, 76, 81
Hollywood, 92
Horses' Glen, 152
House types, 25, 56, 129
Hungry Hill, 133, 139

Inishmurray, 55
Inishowen, 63

Kilcar, 57
Killary Harbour, 28, 32, 33, 36, 41
Killeevy, 116
Killybegs, 57
Kinvarra, 68
Kippure, 91
Knockanaffrin, 123
Knockaunapeebra, 123
Knockcree, 110
Knockdayd (Hungry Hill), 139
Knockmealdown mountains, 119, 120, 125, 129
Knocknapeasta, 151
Knocknarea, 48
Knockshee, 112
Kylemore, 36, 41

Leckavrea Mountain, 42
Legananny, 114
Leinster chain, 89
Lisdoonvarna, 68
Lough Beagh, 63
Lough Callee, 155
Lough Carragh, 154
Lough Conn, 46
Lough Curra, 125

158

INDEX

Lough Dan
Lough Fee, 41
Lough Gouragh, 155
Lough Luggala, 92
Lough Muskry, 126
Lough Nafooey, 43
Lough Shannagh, 111
Lugnaquillia, 15, 89, 97, 114
Lusitanean flora, 18
Lyracappul, 125

Mac Gillycuddy's Reeks, 133, 144, 145, 151
Mass Rocks, 23, 61, 65, 123
Maghera, 112
Malin More, 55, 57
Mangerton, 145, 152
Maumeen, 42
Maumtrasna, 43
Maumturk mountains, 28, 32, 34, 37, 42
Megalithic tombs/culture, 19, 46, 48, 57, 77, 90, 93, 100, 109, 112, 114, 115, 127, 128
Mining, 19, 83, 90, 134, 136
Monavullagh mountains, 120
Money scalp, 26
Mount Brandon, 20, 77, 133, 143, 145, 146, 150, 155
Mount Gabriel, 130
Mount Leinster, 89, 100
Mourne mountains, 89, 102
Muckanaght, 36
Muckish, 62, 63
Mullaghanattin, 144
Mweelrea, 15, 28, 32, 33

Nagles mountains, 128
Nephin, 45, 46
Nephin Beg mountains, 33, 45
North American flora, 18

Oughtmama, 74
Ox mountains, 47

Parknasilla, 135
Partry mountains, 28, 32, 34, 43
Peneplains, 38, 58, 111
Place-names, 26
Poisoned Glen, 63
Pollaphuca, 92

Raths, 19, 64, 73, 76, 136, 146, 149
Red Hugh O'Donnell, 64, 81, 83, 98
Rising of 1798, 65, 91, 99

St. Patrick's Purgatory, 66
Sally Gap, 90, 91
Salruck, 41
Sarsfield, Patrick, 83
Saul, 76, 103
Sawel, 78
Scalp, 93
Scullogue Gap, 100
Seefin, 51
Shan Slieve, 113
Sheeffry Hills, 28, 32, 34
Shehy Mountain, 133, 142, 144
Sherkin Island, 130, 134
Silent Valley, 111
Silvermines, 82, 83
Slane, 77
Slemish, 76
Slieve Anieran, 77, 81
Slieve Aughty, 82, 83
Slieve Bearnagh (Mourne mountains), 102
Slieve Bernagh (Shannon), 82, 83
Slieve Binnian, 103, 110
Slieve Bloom mountains, 76, 82, 87
Slieve Commedagh, 103, 113
Slieve Croob, 104, 114
Slieve Donard, 15, 20, 77, 103, 112
Slieve Elva, 15, 68, 71, 72
Slieve Felim, 82, 84
Slieve Foye (Carlingford Mountain), 117
Slieve Gullion, 76, 114

159

INDEX

Slievekemalta (Keeper Hill), 82, 83
Slieve League, 20, 52, 55, 56, 57, 77

Slieve Meel-More, 103
Slieve Mish, 146, 155
Slieve Miskish, 136, 141
Slieve na Calliagh, 77
Slieve na Goill, 142
Slievenamon, 76, 120
Slieve Reagh, 23, 120, 127, 128
Slieve Snacht, 63
Slieve Tooey, 56, 61
Sligo, 48, 54
Spelga Pass, 111
Sperrin mountains, 76, 78
Sugar Loaf (Slieve na Goill), 139, 142

Teelin, 57
Torc Mountain, 153
Tory Island, 56, 62, 65
Truskmore, 52
Tully Mountain, 32
Twelve Bens, 28, 32, 34, 35, 63, 68

Ulidian (Ulster) cycle of stories, 48, 51, 117

Vinegar Hill, 26

Wicklow Gap, 90, 92
Wicklow mountains, 89
Woods, 19, 71, 73, 83, 153